The "Other" Americans

by
Marcel Gomes Balla

DEDICATION

I would like to dedicate this book to all the Cape Verdeans in America and throughout the world who have been bound together by a common homeland and suffering that has endured for more than five centuries. I would like to give special thanks to Manuel T. Neves, who took the initiative in 1969 and published the first Cape Verdean newspaper in America. This newspaper made many Cape Verdeans aware of their unique heritage for the first time. It was this newspaper that helped me to realize that so much more needs to be done to educate America about the Cape Verdeans in this country. I hope that I have been able to contribute a small effort to what appears to be a monumental task.

ABOUT THE AUTHOR

Marcel Gomes Balla was graduated from Boston University with an MA in International Relations in 1976. He also studied at the University of Lisbon in Portugal. He has served abroad as an International Community Development Consultant, speaks six languages and has written many articles on the history of Cabo Verde.

THE "OTHER" AMERICANS

A book about the forgotten people in America who played a key role in the discovery of the New World.

ISBN 0-89288-214-X

Maverick Publications, Inc.
P. O. Box 5007
Bend, Oregon • 97708

Contents

APPENDICES

PREFACE

I strongly believe that the Cape Verdean people are the most neglected minority group in America. Despite the incredible achievements of this small group, historians and the United States Government have consistently ignored them.

Now, for the first time, I have decided to inform America about our rich cultural heritage so that all Americans will know that we exist as a united and proud people. The next time someone asks, "What is a Cape Verdean?" just tell him to read this book. Almost all Americans will be shocked to learn the truth about Cape Verdeans and their homeland.

As the world prepares to celebrate the 500th anniversary of the discovery of the new world in 1992, this book will offer some amazing revelations that have been ignored for centuries. No educated American can afford to be without this book.

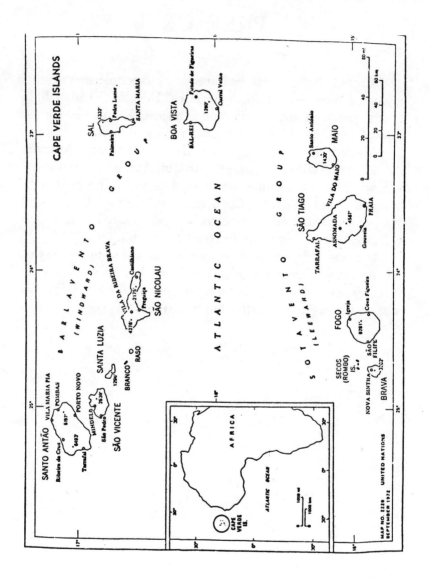

CAPE VERDE ISLANDS

SANTO ANTÃO

VILA MARIA PIA

Ribeira da Cruz · POMBAS

· 2407
Tarrafal ·
· 5187
PORTO NOVO

MINDELO
São Pedro · 2639
SÃO VICENTE

SANTA LUZIA

· 1290
BRANCO
RASO

B A R L A V E N T O
(W I N D W A R D)

G R O U P

SAL
· 1337
Palmeira ·
Pedra Lume ·
SANTA MARIA

BOA VISTA
SAL-REI ·
· 1290
Curral Velho

VILA DA RIBEIRA BRAVA
· 2175
Praguiça
· 4278
SÃO NICOLAU
Castilhano

Santo Antônio ·
· 1430
MAIO
VILA DO MAIO

A T L A N T I C   O C E A N

S O T A V E N T O
(L E E W A R D)

G R O U P

SÃO TIAGO
TARRAFAL ·
ASSOMADA
· 456
Gouveia ·
PRAIA

FOGO
Igreja ·
Cova Figueira
· 9281
SÃO FILIPE · 2827
SECOS (ROMBO) IS.
NOVA SINTRA ·
BRAVA

AFRICA

ATLANTIC OCEAN

CAPE VERDE IS.

1000 mi
1000 km

SEPTEMBER 1972

50 mi
0 20 40 60
0 20 40 60 km

INTRODUCTION

This book is written for the American people who are unaware of the Cape Verdeans who live in this country and the role that these people played in the discovery of America. It is also meant to inform the Cape Verdean people of America of their unique heritage and culture so that they can better understand themselves and contribute to the development of further studies about Cape Verde and the Cape Verdean people.

This book should be of particular interest to all schools in America, both public and private, including colleges and universities. This is especially true if we are going to celebrate the 500th anniversary of Columbus' discovery of America in 1992.

I have also tried to portray the everyday life of the islands, particularly Brava, which should be of interest to Cape Verdeans in America who have never been to their homeland. Many Cape Verdean Americans take life in the U.S. for granted. Perhaps they will be able to re-evaluate their outlook and take a more constructive role in their history.

All other Americans should re-evaluate their treatment of U.S. Cape Verdeans. Racial policies should also be re-evaluated in America. Recently, I tuned in to the "Geraldo" TV show, and he expressed a deep concern that America's racial policies are the basis for destroying this country. I am convinced that this is true. Hopefully, the readers of this book will get a better understanding of all people of this world and try to find a way to bridge the gap between different peoples before it destroys a great nation.

A BRIEF HISTORY OF CABO VERDE

In order to introduce the reader to the Cape Verdean people and a better understanding of this book, I believe that it is essential that people around the world and especially in the United States of America understand the history of Cabo Verde and its people. This history is almost completely ignored by America and Americans. Our history has been ignored more than any other cultural group in America.

Most Americans have heard of Blacks, Arabs, Hispanics, Asians and Indians, but practically no one has heard of Cape Verdeans unless they have lived in or near a Cape Verdean community. Chances are that for those who have heard of Cape Verdeans, they know almost nothing about the history and geography of this much neglected group.

Therefore, based upon these assumptions, I am going to attempt to identify the land and its people so that Cape Verdeans in America and around the world can stand up and be counted with pride and dignity.

Three navigators have claimed to be the discoverer of the Cape Verde Islands: Alvise da Cadamosto (Venetian) in 1456, Diogo Gomes (Portuguese) and Antonio da Noli (Genovese) in either 1458 or 1460. All three were in the service of Prince Henry the Navigator of Portugal. According to the experts, it seems as though da Noli has the best claim, because he was awarded a captaincy on the island of Sao Tiago as a direct result of his claim. King Manuel declared in a letter of 8 April 1497, that da Noli was the discoverer and colonizer of Sao Tiago and was rewarded with a captaincy for part of it.

Antonio da Noli settled with his brother Bartholomew and nephew Raphael at Ribeira Grande and founded the first township on Sao Tiago circa 1462. The first Christian Cathedral outside the "old world" of Europe and the Middle East was also constructed here. Today, its ruins are a tourist attraction.

Antonio da Noli's name also appears on Italian maps as the discoverer of the islands. Based on available evidence, it seems as though da Noli has received most of the recognition as the discoverer.

These islands are also considered to have been the last important discovery of Prince Henry the Navigator, who is regarded by historians as the greatest figure in the history of exploration.

The evolution of the Cape Verdean people began shortly after the first settlement, when Africans were introduced to the islands. I discuss this subject in more detail in another chapter.

The official name of the country is The "Republic of Cape Verde." In Portuguese it is "Republica de Cabo Verde." The President is Aristides Pereira, who was chosen in 1975 after independence from Portugal. General Pedro Pires is the Premier and was chosen to this post also in 1975. The government is run by the fifty-six-member body called the National Assembly and they have close ties with other former Portuguese colonies who became independent at about the same time.

Geographically, it is 1,557 square miles in area, about the size of Rhode Island. The country is an island nation that consists of ten main islands located at 16° N latitude and 23° W longitude; about 400 miles west of Dakar, Senegal and 1,000 miles east of Brazil. The islands are composed of two groups: Barlavento in the north, which consists of Santa Antao (291 square miles), Boa Vista (240 square miles), Sao Nicolau (132 square miles), Sao Vicente (88 square miles), Sal (83 square miles), and Santa Luzia (13 square miles); and Sotavento in the south, which consists of Sao Tiago (383 square miles), Fogo (184 square miles), Maio (103 square miles), and Brava (25 square miles). The islands are mostly mountainous and of volcanic origin. The island of Fogo still has one of the world's few active volcanoes.

The islands are deeply scarred by erosion and the country suffers from lack of sufficient rainfall to meet the needs of the people.

The largest city is Mindelo on Sao Vicente with a population of about 50,000 inhabitants. However, Praia, the capital city located on Sao Tiago, was quickly approaching the size of

Mindelo and may have already surpassed it as more and more people flock to the capital in search of jobs, education and health care.

The people are mostly Catholic, but other Christian religions do exist. Most of the people are poor but progress is seen throughout the country. The people have been basically ignored in the past by the western powers as Portugal was responsible for its economic development and that didn't bode well for the Cape Verdeans and thus came the revolution, and finally independence on July 5th, 1975. Economic and political relations with Portugal have been positive since independence and one can find Portuguese investment projects throughout the islands. Portuguese is the national language and thus there is strong rapport with all other Portuguese-speaking countries, including Portugal.

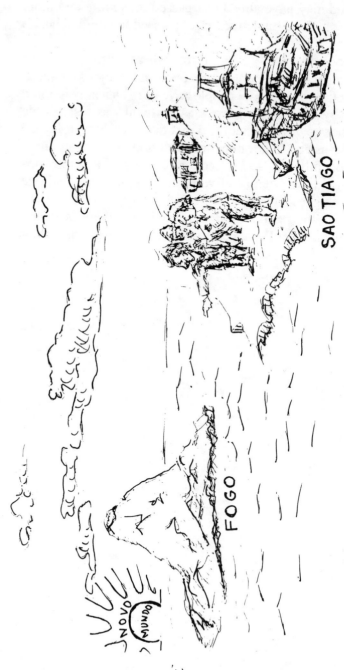

CAPE VERDEANS Showing Columbus the route to
THE NEW WORLD ~ July 1498

FOGO

SAO TIAGO

NOVO MUNDO

© Marcel Gomes Balla July 1990

THE DISCOVERY OF AMERICA AND THE CAPE VERDE CONNECTION

Apparently there is a strong connection between Columbus and the Atlantic islands of Madeira, the Canary Islands and the Cape Verde Islands. Few people realize that prior to 1492, Columbus had lived in Madeira for a few years and because of the close proximity to the Canary Islands, he must have been aware of these islands also, since he had sailed southward along the African coast. More important, however, was the fact that he made voyages with the Portuguese, who possessed the Cape Verde Islands and claimed Guinea as a possession of Portugal. This period of Columbus is probably between 1476 and 1485. In 1479, he married a Portuguese woman from a royal family, Dona Felipa, and took up residency in Porto Santo, a small island about 40 miles off the main island of Madeira in the Madeira Archipelago. He is believed to have made several voyages from Madeira during this period. The most logical destinations would have been the Cape Verde Islands and Guinea, since these were claimed by Portugal. He may have sailed to the Canary Islands also, but at this time these islands belonged to Spain (at one time they had belonged to Portugal), but some of the islands were still being contested.

Columbus himself tells us in his log (during his discovery voyage to America) of Saturday, September 29, 1492, that he saw a frigate bird and that he had seen many of them before when he was in the Cape Verde Islands.

It is believed that Columbus wanted to sail to America (in his theory it would have been India) in 1484, while in the service of Portugal. He approached King John on this matter, but was turned down because of demands that were considered to be too high a price for the king to pay. However, it is further believed that the King's councilors advised him to take advantage of Columbus' ideas without paying him his price.

From this episode, some say, a caravel was secretly sent from the Cape Verde Islands and actually sailed westward for several days before giving up and returning to Lisbon.

One thing is clear and that is that Columbus was in the Cape Verde Islands on his third voyage to America in 1498. He anchored in Boa Vista from June 27-30, 1498, and on July 5, 1498, was in Sao Tiago, which had a considerable settlement of Portuguese and their African subjects. He found the Cape Verde Islands dry and sterile, not verdant.

In fact, it has been said that when Columbus arrived in Cape Verde in 1498, he said that the name Cape Verde was a false name, "falso nombre," because it was so dry that he couldn't see anything green there. He also found everybody to be sick and he didn't want to stay among them (this was probably in reference to the lepers who went to Cape Verde to be cured). Columbus also didn't like the name Boa Vista, which means "nice view." When he arrived there he found the island to be very sterile and barren.

Many people have wondered why the islands were so named and it is difficult to find a historical answer to this puzzle. I have personally heard some people say that it was green when first discovered and then livestock, especially goats, were introduced to the islands and they eventually consumed all the green vegetation. Despite this problem, I have found at least one statement that claims that the islands were, in fact, called the Cape Verde Islands because of their beautiful verdure when first discovered (Reference an English map that was published January 1, 1770). I also suspect that if there was a good rainfall on the islands just before they were discovered, then it is possible that they were green at the time of discovery. Certainly, most people know that the islands are usually dry and barren because of the lack of rainfall. I understand, however, that they do turn green after a healthy rainfall (this may not be true of all islands).

Some of the inhabitants of Cape Verde had told Columbus of a mysterious island that appeared southwesterly of Fogo (Cape Verde Islands) and which King John II had planned to discover. They also claimed that canoes filled with merchandise from the west coast of Africa had been seen heading in that direction. So, when Columbus passed Fogo after leaving Sao

Tiago, he wanted to test the theory of the Cape Verdean residents and the King of Portugal, i.e., discover a mainland to the south. In fact, this is exactly what Columbus did, and he landed in the vicinity of Trinidad and Venezuela. This was extremely significant because it was the first time that Columbus reached the American continent. Prior to this discovery he had only found some Caribbean islands.

Two years later Pedro Alvarez Cabral discovered Brazil in 1500, after stopping over in the Cape Verde Islands. It is also of historical significance that Cabral deliberately stopped in Cabo Verde in the year 1500, on the island of Sao Tiago, to plan the details of his "official" discovery of Brazil. This is a previously unpublished fact that was established by the internationally renowned Portuguese historian, Dr. Jose de Braganca in his book *Terra Grande*. Let us not forget that the Cape Verdeans were well aware of the "Novo Continente" or new continent, so this was the ideal location for planning such an adventure. What is perhaps interesting about all of this is that the Cape Verde Islands seem to be a focal point along the route of discoveries to America and India, but almost nothing is said about the Cape Verdean people at this time except for a few words by Samuel Eliot Morison, who states that the islands were used for the lepers who were supposed to be cured by eating turtle meat and bathing in turtle blood on the islands of Boa Vista and Sao Tiago. It is also Morison who speaks of the Portuguese settlements and their African subjects, mentioned previously.

Despite the problems of gathering historical information, it is still possible to do so. We are fortunate that at least one historian, Dr. D. W. Meinig has recently written a very detailed book, *The Shaping of America*, in which he dramatically revises history as we once knew it. This book will go down in history as a monumental undertaking in an attempt to tell the truth about historical events and the people who made them possible.

On the issue of race, Dr. Meinig explains the problems of racial classification, which is seen as offensive to some ethnic groups. He states that we must try to be sensitive to such concerns, but believes that such classifications cannot be avoided. What he suggests is that we acknowledge the presence of all races as participants in our national history and to under-

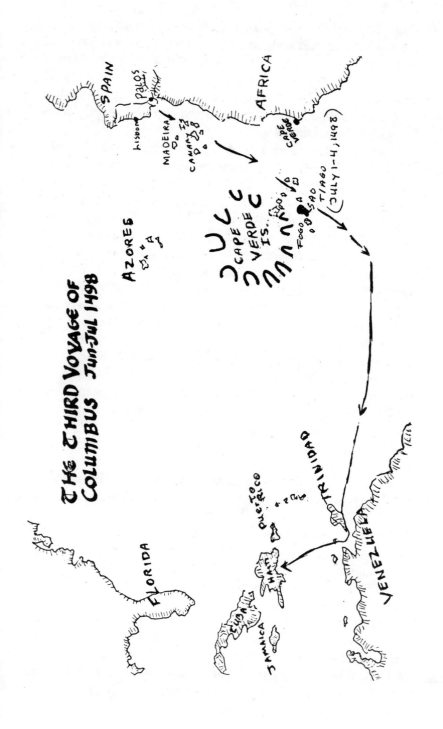

The THIRD VOYAGE OF COLUMBUS Jun–Jul 1498

SPAIN
PALOS
LISBON
MADEIRA
CANARY IS.
AFRICA
CAPE VERDE
(JULY 1-4, 1498)
AZORES
CAPE VERDE IS.
TIAGO
FOGO
SAO
FLORIDA
CUBA
JAMAICA
HAITI
PUERTO RICO
TRINIDAD
VENEZUELA

stand that there are seventy to eighty different ethnic groups in America and not just the seven or eight that predominate our literature.

Dr. Meinig offers some very revealing descriptions about Cape Verdeans in the 15th and 16th centuries. I discuss this subject in more detail in the next chapter. In the meantime, he observes that historians, who do not understand Africans and others, have tried to gather evidence and interpret their history, rather than allow these people to write their own history based on their own understanding of events. In effect, he tells us that we are dependent upon history written by whites that graphically distorts the true interpretations of events and peoples. This message is a new one to America in preparation for the 500-year history celebration coming up in 1992.

For those readers who would like more specific information about Columbus in Cape Verde, he anchored at Porto Sal Rei, on the island of Boa Vista, with the flagships *Vaquero* and *Correo*, where he met with D. Rodrigo Alfonzo, the Cape Verdean captain of the island. On the island of Sao Tiago, he anchored at Ribeira Grande. I recommend that Samuel Eliot Morison's books be read for further study. I have listed a couple of them in the appendix.

In 1466, Alfonso V of Portugal granted the inhabitants on the island of Sao Tiago the right to engage in trade with Guinea. Guinea, it must be remembered, had been discovered by Portugal much earlier. So the inhabitants had the right to trade for slaves and other goods with Guinea, which increased the population and wealth of Cape Verde. In 1495, Cape Verde became a part of Portugal.

Madeira, the Azores and the Cape Verde Islands were all colonized in the 15th century by Portugal and it is common for these islands to be recognized as stepping stones to the new world. Yet, as Dr. D. W. Meinig tells us in his book, *The Shaping of America*, these islands were much more than stations to the new world. They were, in fact, themselves a new world and important proving grounds for new seafaring and planting systems. These settlers were the pioneers in a New World.

Hopefully, every student and educator in America will understand that the people from Madeira, the Azores and the Cape

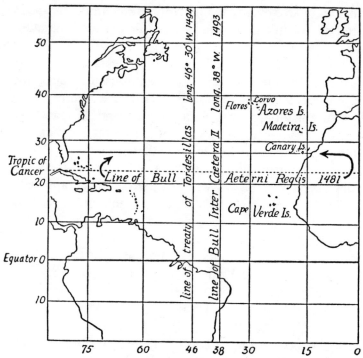

THE LINES OF DEMARCATION BETWEEN
SPAIN AND PORTUGAL

ONE HALF TO PORTUGAL, ONE HALF TO SPAIN: THE TREATY OF TORDESILLAS DIVIDES THE WORLD

Verde Islands were the pioneers in a new world. This is a fundamental fact of history and clearly documented. Isn't it time that America recognizes this historical truth?

One of the most intriguing subjects in the discovery of the New World has to be the Treaty of Tordesillas. It was this treaty that was sponsored by the Pope in 1494 that divided the world of discoveries between Spain and Portugal. In 1493, a papal bull was drawn up to partition the world between Spain and Portugal, based upon the location of the Cape Verde Islands, i.e., any land that was beyond a demarcation line of 100 leagues west of the Cape Verdes would belong to Spain and everything east of that line would go to Portugal. This agreement was not working well and in 1494 King John wanted a new agreement that gave Portugal everything 370 leagues east of the demarcation line.

King John was firm in his negotiations in 1494 and was awarded all lands 370 leagues (1,200 miles) east of the demarcation line. In effect this meant that Brazil would eventually come under Portuguese control. The significance of this treaty is the fact that in 1494 it appears that King John was already aware of the South American continent and planned to discover it before the Spanish. So it can be said that half the people of South America are speaking Portuguese today because of the historical role of Cape Verde in the Treaty of Tordesillas in 1494. It is equally significant to say that the other half of South America is Spanish-speaking because of the same treaty.

Another very important benefit of this treaty was the fact that Portugal gained control of the eastern markets which included India (East Indies) as well as Africa. It actually seems incredible today that a nation of probably less than a million people could have had such influence in the world.

Once again the Cape Verde Islands played a major role in the Portuguese Empire. It was here in July and August 1497 that Vasco da Gama came, enroute to India. While in the Cape Verde Islands, he made final adjustments to his ships and received provisions for the long journey. This was very important because he would be taking a route of 4,000 miles before he would see land again. So this was considered to be a "crucial leg" of his journey to India and it was here that he prepared his crew for the journey ahead. On 3 Aug. 1497, he sailed from the bay of Santa Maria on the island of Sao Tiago and headed for India. It was this voyage that enabled Portugal to establish Europe's first great link with the orient and gave her control of this commercial trade which lasted for more than two centuries.

On the issue of the Portuguese Empire, I think that it is essential that the world understand how a small nation could manage such a huge responsibility. I believe that there were three major ingredients that made this possible: (1) A friendship treaty with England that dates back to the 14th century and the oldest of its kind in the world. Since England was the dominant sea power in the world, it was certainly nice for Portugal to have such a friend as a benefactor if needed. (2) The Cape Verde Islands and its people, a largely mulatto population that could adjust to tropical climates much easier than Europeans, while communicating in Portuguese, Crioulo and African dialects. This unique combination of a racial mix and a linguistic aptitude proved invaluable because of Portugal's interaction with Africans and other races. The strategic location of the Cape Verde Islands and the people made it practically an empire within an empire, or a Cape Verdean Empire within the Portuguese Empire. (3) Finally, there were the Portuguese themselves, who were very open to the idea of miscegenation and multiplying the Portuguese peoples for the purpose of extending their dominion over the world. Along with their navigational skills, these three ingredients formed an awesome power structure that literally changed the course of world history. To better understand these key points, one only has to look at Brazil and glance at their ethnicity, culture and economy, which were largely influenced directly by Africans who came by way of Cape Verde. The Cape Verdeans also christianized the Africans, which added even more influence to the empire with the blessings of the church.

In discussions about the Cape Verde Islands and the efforts to discover a new sea route to India, much is rumored about the secrecy of Portugal. Many historians seem to agree that Portugal had secret information and was very protective of this knowledge so that it wouldn't get in the hands of foreign powers. However, now that 1992 is upon us, it would seem to be natural for the Portuguese government to disclose any information if, in fact, they have any, that would support or refute any arguments concerning the discovery of America. Of particular interest would be any disclosures that describe the people who inhabited the Madeira Islands and the Cape Verde Islands.

Cape Verde was a major calling port during the Age of Discovery and ships would often rest their crews and get food supplies such as livestock and water. This practice caused great concern among sea captains because many mariners would desert the ships and stay on the islands rather than continue a long journey that seemed to be getting further and further away. Obviously, with ships passing from Portugal and Spain in the first years of the discoveries and then eventually from England and other European countries, several nationalities would settle on the islands. Since there were also many African slaves on the islands, the gradual evolution of the Cape Verdean people was being formed.

Under these conditions, it would seem that Cape Verdeans must have come to America during a key phase of the "Discovery" years. Some historians even have good reason to believe that Cape Verdeans may have introduced bananas to the New World prior to the discovery of America by Columbus.

Cape Verdeans have a right to know their history and America should be aware of these people who have lived on her soil for centuries without recognition as a unique people. Now is the time to open the doors for America's least recognized cultural group—The "Other" Americans—who were the first settlers in the New World.

REQUEST FOR RACIAL AND ETHNIC DATA

This information is requested solely for the purpose of determining compliance with federal civil rights law, and your response will not affect consideration of your application. By providing this information you will assist us in assuring that the Peace Corps is administered in a nondiscriminatory manner.

The information requested on this section is covered by the provisions of the Privacy Act as stated on the inside cover of this application.

Instructions: please categorize yourself by placing an "x" in the box next to the proper category.

☐ Black, not of Hispanic origin (a person having origins in any of the Black racial groups of Africa). (1)

☐ Hispanic (a person of Mexican, Puerto Rican, Cuban, Central or South American or other Spanish culture or origin, regardless of race). (2)

☐ American Indian or Alaskan Native (a person having origins in any of the original peoples of North America, and who maintains cultural identification through tribal affiliation or community recognition). (3)

☐ Asian or Pacific Islander (a person having origins in any of the original peoples of the Far East, Southeast Asia, the Indian subcontinent, or the Pacific islands. This area includes, for example, China, India, Japan, Korea, the Philippines, Samoa, and Viet Nam). (4)

☐ White, not of Hispanic origin (having origins in any of the original peoples of Europe, North Africa, or the Middle East). (7)

☐ I prefer not to respond. (8)

IMPORTANT

There is no discrimination on account of race, color, national origin, age, handicap, political belief, sex, or religion. All services are administered on a non-discriminatory basis. Anyone who feels he/she has been discriminated against may write to the Peace Corps, Office of Compliance, Washington, D.C. 20526.

On this form even the term "other" is omitted so Cape Verdeans are clearly eliminated from the competition. In the meantime, Vietnamese and Koreans are recognized, which gives them a distinct advantage over Cape Verdeans, who have been here for centuries longer. It is impossible for Cape Verdeans to understand this official bias. It appears that the federal policy is to force the Cape Verdeans out of the country that they have supported and defended. This policy is the basis for the psychological breakdown of the family, and the destruction of the Cape Verdean society as a whole. It is for this reason that Cape Verdeans *must* be united before a glorious heritage becomes extinct. This policy appears to be pushing the Cape Verdeans towards extinction and third class citizenship (behind anglos and recognized minorities), in a nation that preaches "equal rights for all."

AMERICA'S IGNORANCE OF
CAPE VERDE

To better understand the ignorance of Americans, one only has to look at any federal employment form and try to find the ethnic group designation for Cape Verdeans. It is strange to know that Eskimos and Indians are listed, along with Asians, Blacks and Hispanics, but nowhere on any federal form will one find a place for Cape Verdeans, despite the achievements that these people have made in America.

The Cape Verdean people developed the Ocean Spray Cranberry Company in Onset, Massachusetts; they were the whalers in Herman Melville's great novel, *Moby Dick*; they have achieved outstanding levels in boxing, baseball, basketball, football and track. Some of the greatest athletes and coaches in America are Cape Verdeans. Cape Verdean musicians have played with the great bands of Count Basie and other outstanding bands.

I can still remember the cranberry bogs as a child. I must have seen thousands of cranberry pickers, including children and elderly men and women, and to the best of my knowledge, I don't remember seeing any cranberry picker *who was not a Cape Verdean*. The irony of this story is that in the town of Wareham, Massachusetts, there was a sign posted on Route 28 at the entrance to the town that stated proudly, "You are now entering Wareham, the Cranberry Capital of the World." How true it was, we represented the cranberry capital of the world and surely we must have been the world's greatest cranberry pickers, but who got the big money and the credit for our efforts? The town of Wareham, Massachusetts. Which company represented the biggest profiteers? The Ocean Spray Cranberry Corporation. Who did the labor? The Cape Verdeans. We made the Ocean Spray Cranberry Corporation what it is today. Isn't it ironic that practically every American has heard of Ocean Spray Cranberry juice, and almost no one has heard of Cape Verdeans?

If America is so proud of her cranberries, why is she so ashamed of the Cape Verdeans? Well, hopefully, every Cape Verdean in America will tell the world who we are before the end of 1992.

The U.S. Government has finally made restitution to the Japanese-Americans for the disgrace that these noble Americans suffered during World War II, now they should mandate a directive to educate every American about Cape Verdeans for the disgrace we have suffered in this country. Every Cape Verdean parent and non-Cape Verdean alike, should demand from their school district that Cape Verdean history be a mandatory subject, especially in Boston, New Bedford, Wareham and Cape Cod, Massachusetts; Providence and Pawtucket, Rhode Island; and Sacramento and Los Angeles, California.

There is absolutely no logical reason why Cape Verdean taxpayers should pay to have their children learn about Europeans in American History and not about Cape Verdeans in American History. We all know that the Bostonian's battle cry during the famous Boston Tea Party was "No taxation without representation." Naturally, they blamed the uprising on the Indians. If they were proud of this, then we should be willing to stand up and *refuse* to pay taxes for education until we are duly represented in the system.

If it is true that man is the product of his environment, then clearly most Cape Verdeans have had to survive a very discriminatory environment. Perhaps a special study is needed to determine the socio-economic effects of the Cape Verdean society that have resulted from this situation.

So I believe that it is time for all Americans to wake up and give credit for the achievements made by Cape Verdeans so that all America can benefit. This is especially true because of our mixed racial heritage where everybody is treated by one another as basically the same despite the difference in our skin tone.

America can learn a lot from observing and studying the history of the Cape Verdean people, then maybe many of the traditional racial barriers will break down and disappear. What is a logical and natural attitude on the issue of racial differences for Cape Verdeans, becomes an almost impossible dilemma for typical Americans to solve, which in turn is leading the country backwards and toward third-world status as a direct result of ignorance.

It is important to understand that Cape Verde was initially uninhabited and eventually was settled by the Portuguese, who used the islands as slave trading stations for the export of slaves to Latin America. Unfortunately, this represents a darker side of Cape Verdean history. According to folklore, it was also used for prisoners and other "undesirables" who were evicted from Portugal prior to the onset of the slave trade between Africa and Latin America.

The details of the slave trade will offer a fascinating insight into the Portuguese mind as well as that of Cape Verdeans. One can only wonder how the Cape Verdeans could have dealt with this trade. Believe it or not, this subject is given radical treatment in *The Shaping of America*. In this work, you will find some startling revelations about how Cape Verdeans altered the course of world history forever.

Dr. Meinig clearly establishes that Cape Verdeans (who were "called" Portuguese in the beginning) were rapidly becoming a mulatto race of people at the end of the 15th century. This was so because Portuguese families were not attracted to these islands as they were to the Azores and Madeira. The Portuguese and other European men, especially Italians and Castilians, formed a "cultural fusion" with the African peoples. Ironically, this fusion resulted in what Dr. Meinig calls the first Africanization of a European society. It also gave the Cape Verdeans the extraordinary ability to deal directly with Africans and others on behalf of Portugal. In effect, Cape Verde and the Cape Verdeans became the glue that held the Portuguese Empire together for several centuries and changed the course of world history on four continents—Africa, America, Asia and Europe.

If you are a Cape Verdean, then I strongly urge you to read his book, which is listed in the reference section. However, you must be prepared to learn about the *bad* as well as the good about our history, and so you should read it with an open mind. This book is very important to all Cape Verdeans who truly want to understand how we got into our dilemma in the first place.

We can blame Portugal or America, or both, for our problems, if we so choose, but in the end we must depend on ourselves to resolve them. The best statement that I can make on this subject is that we must learn from the past but we can no longer live in the past if we wish to succeed in a modern world. Yet, we can see from the past that we have enormous potential as a people, despite our small population. We simply must learn to adapt to the realities of a modern world. *In other words, we must awaken ourselves to a new era, otherwise we will find ourselves trapped forever.*

Most of the Portuguese who came to Cape Verde are believed to have come from the southern part of Portugal and from Madeira (a group of islands that belong to Portugal, which is located in the vicinity of the Canary Islands off the northwest coast of Africa). Other ethnic groups have also settled on the islands and, after 500 years of evolution, the population has merged into a mixed racial group which has been called "mestizo" or "crioulo." In America, it is common for Cape Verdeans to be called Portygee (pronounced port-ee-gee [hard g]), which seems to be used to distinguish the Cape Verdeans from the Portuguese from Portugal. Usually the Cape Verdean people refer to one another as Crioulos (sometimes spelled 'Creoles') and in recent years many people refer to themselves as Cape Verdeans.

Since I grew up in a Cape Verdean community on Cape Cod in Massachusetts, I could never understand why we didn't have any history in textbooks in our school system. Everybody seemed to be from the "Old Country" (our term for Cabo Verde), but I don't remember anyone who actually was able or willing to locate it on a map. We had our own language, culture and ethnicity, and the school system treated us as though we were different and didn't belong in the traditional American society. Personally, I don't believe that any of the teachers had any idea who we were or where Cabo Verde was located.

It was clear that the school system and the local government and civic organizations discriminated against the Cape Verdean people, but it was very difficult for the Cape Verdeans to understand this strange behavior. It was difficult to understand because most Cape Verdeans got along well with the other local citizens in school and church and so forth.

Some Cape Verdeans even developed close friendships with many of the local townspeople irregardless of their ethnicity. Although most Cape Verdeans mingled freely with everyone in public, in private it was usually a different story. For example, it was common in many Cape Verdean neighborhoods for the people to mix freely with one another and to be treated as a member of the family in a neighbor's house. This rarely ever happened in non-Cape Verdean neighborhoods. Racial remarks were seldom made publicly and although racism was discussed, the Cape Verdeans usually did so only with other Cape Verdeans. In those days, back in the '40s and '50s, it was considered to be impolite for Cape Verdeans to discuss racial issues or to make racial remarks with non-Cape Verdeans. This attitude seemed to be prevalent throughout the local area, in spite of one's racial background.

So, generally speaking, everything seemed to be okay on the surface, however it was clear that Cape Verdeans were given all the menial jobs and very few were ever considered for professional jobs. It was also clear that Cape Verdeans were not represented in local politics and always depended on non-Cape Verdeans for their wages and livelihood.

Many Cape Verdeans actually owned their own homes, because it was common for Cape Verdeans to help one another. People, usually family members, would help one another to build a home and many of their friends would join them. Of course, many of them would be paid if it was possible, but it was also common for kids to help out in exchange for a good meal and perhaps some pocket change. Others would probably do it as a favor in exchange for another favor.

So it is in this background that I decided to learn more about my roots and travel to the "Old Country." I had traveled around the world many times as a result of my military service between 1956 and 1977, but I never had the opportunity to visit Cabo Verde. However, in 1986, I was working in Belgium and discovered many Cape Verdean communities in the Benelux countries, i.e., Belgium, the Netherlands and Luxembourg. There was also a schedule of flights going direct to the islands. I also realized that I had an aunt who lived in the "Old Country," but whom I hadn't contacted for nearly 10 years.

Of course, I wasn't even sure if she was still alive because I knew she would be over 80 years old. Nevertheless, I wrote her a letter and a few weeks later I received a reply, and I was obviously overjoyed to find that she was alive and well at the age of 82. At that moment I decided once and for all to visit her because I wouldn't have many more opportunities if any at all.

So finally I made preparations for my trip to Cabo Verde and in June 1986 I purchased my ticket from a Cape Verdean travel agency in Rotterdam, Holland. These were very exciting times for me, as the travel agency took care of all the formalities for me and did everything possible to make it an unforgettable journey into history and time. Somehow, I felt like I was entering into a time machine as I boarded the plane to Rotterdam destined for Cabo Verde on June 27th, 1986.

MY ARRIVAL IN THE "OLD COUNTRY"

I arrived in Sal at about 10:00 p.m. Cape Verdean time on 27 June 1986 and waited at the airport about 5 hours for a plane to Praia (the capital of the Cape Verde Islands). I arrived in Praia at about 5:30 a.m. on 28 June 1986, after a one-hour flight from Sal. I took a taxi with Olavo (my new friend whom I met on the plane) to the hotel Casa Felicidades. Although we got a room without too much difficulty, we had to get up after only three hours sleep because we would have to go to the travel agency and confirm our flight reservations back to Sal. It didn't take long for me to realize that travel arrangements should be confirmed as soon as possible, especially during the busy seasons.

While my destination was to reach the island of Brava, I learned that I would have to remain in Praia for three days while awaiting travel connections to Brava. During my stay in Praia I met many interesting people. I learned also that I had cousins in Praia that I didn't even know existed. Otavo Silva was one such cousin. He worked in a hardware store and looked to be about 35 years old. I didn't know it at the time, but I had a first cousin named Belmiro Balla, who died a few years earlier at the age of 69 and who is believed to be the father of about 40 children on several of the islands. Otavo was one of these cousins fathered by Belmiro.

Since I was usually with Olavo, it was easy to meet new friends in Praia, because Olavo was a frequent traveler around the islands who worked and lived in Europe several months a year. Fortunately for me, Olavo also knew my relatives and this proved to be very helpful on many occasions.

I also met Mr. George Miranda, the head of the government-owned bookstore and a cousin of Mr. Jorge Barboza, a friend of mine who was an administrator in Louvain, the well-known Belgian university. Another cousin of Mr. Barboza was Mr. George Leitao, who appeared to be an influential state official who had offices in the Ministry of Health as well as the Brazilian Embassy. Mr. Leitao was very friendly and invited me to his home, which was a beautiful house in a new development on the edge of Praia. At his home I met his charming wife and Mr. Elizio Fernandes, who was the manager of the Cape Verdean Bank. Mr. Fernandes invited me to visit him at the bank after my visit to Brava and upon my return to Praia, since I would have to return to Praia for my travel connections.

On the way back to the hotel, Mr. Leitao drove his car and showed me the local sites of interest. The main attraction was definitely the visit to the Palacio de Congreso. Here, Mr. Leitao showed me an exposition presented in honor of the 10th anniversary of the Bank of Cape Verde. He also informed me that the Chinese provided all the materials for the building, which was surprisingly very elaborate and well constructed. Nevertheless, the Cape Verdeans provided the labor. It was obvious that Mr. Leitao was very proud of this project. This was a very natural sentiment and easily understood by anyone who was aware of the colonial times when Cape Verde was ruled by Portugal. During the colonial days, such an elaborate building was unthinkable. Now progress was being made and the citizens were showing their new pride.

I finally returned to the hotel and, after a good night's sleep, I awoke at 4:30 a.m. and at 5:00 a.m. the cab driver arrived to take me to the airport for my flight to Fogo. I had made previous arrangements with the cab driver to pick me up at 5:00 a.m. In order to get to Brava I would have to take a plane to Fogo and eventually take a boat to Brava, since the airport in Brava was barely under construction and probably would not be ready for at least a year.

At any rate, the cab driver charged me 300$00 escudos, although the hotel clerk told me that the fare should be about 100$00 escudos. A couple from Sao Tome paid 200$00 escudos for the exact same trip from the same hotel with another cab and they also were picked up at 5:00 a.m.

The airport was not open when I arrived. The travel agency had informed me to be there at 5:45 a.m. (one hour before flight time). It was about 5:15 a.m. when I arrived, so I chatted with the couple from Sao Tome. At first I was surprised by the fluency in Portuguese until they explained that they were from Sao Tome (also a former Portuguese island colony, as was Cape Verde). They were also surprised at my fluency in Portuguese, especially since I was charged 300$00 escudos by the cab driver. They told me that Sao Tome was about a four or five hour flight from the island of Sal, and that it always rained there. They seemed to think that the cost of living in the Cape Verde Islands was pretty high.

The airport terminal opened up at about 6:00 a.m. All passengers for the flight to Fogo were checked in and we had to stand on a scale to get weighed. It seemed as though some people had priority during the in-processing procedures. I never did understand that. By this time my friend Olavo had already joined me and was my travel guide during my travel arrangements, since he was also going to the same village, as his family also lived in Nova Sintra on the island of Brava.

Finally, we were given a boarding pass and then we lined up at the boarding gate to get on the plane. The luggage preceded the passengers and then everybody got on board the aircraft, a small plane with about 18 seats. Everything appeared to be okay, as the pilots started to crank up the engine, but after 10 minutes or so, it was obvious that there was a problem. It seemed as though the engine lacked the power to take off. Anyway, the pilot asked everyone to return to the terminal while they (two pilots) corrected the technical problem. Nearly two hours later, we were advised to leave the terminal and return at 2:30 p.m., as the flight would be rescheduled to leave at 3:30 p.m. Many people left by taxi, but a few people remained, including myself. There really wasn't any place for me to go now, except to Fogo.

This situation caused some confusion, because several women had young children and babies to watch. Fortunately for me at least, there was a tiny snack bar upstairs with a few tables, where I managed to get a couple of sandwiches and a bottle of mineral water.

In the meantime, it seemed as though other flights to other islands were going smoothly. Later in the afternoon, two of my traveling friends (a couple of young girls) from Rotterdam, came into the terminal with some of their relatives whom they were visiting in Praia. Although we had arrived together in Praia three days earlier, we had lost contact during our stay in the city, so we were surprised to meet again. Naturally we took advantage of this opportunity to chat for a few minutes.

Carlita, one of my friends, told me that her relatives lived in Santa Caterina, which was about an hour from Praia, and since she was staying with them, she was not in Praia, and that's the reason that I hadn't seen them. My friends were planning to visit the island of Sao Vincent and returning later to Praia. So, after our friendly reunion, we parted company with the hope that we would reunite in Praia within a couple of weeks. Fortunately, seeing my friends turned out to be a pleasant experience after a difficult day of inconsistencies.

At 2:30 p.m. the passengers for our delayed flight to Fogo started arriving (again). There still weren't any visible signs that our flight would be departing at 3:30, the latest schedule. Then, after more confusion, we were given another boarding pass (the first pass was torn up by the stewardess when we boarded the plane earlier in the day). It was about 4:30 p.m. when we eventually boarded the plane and we took off at 4:45 p.m. for Sao Felipe, the capital of Fogo.

It seemed a little strange at first, that we were finally airborne, after all the problems we encountered during the day. In fairness to the pilots, it was a very pleasant flight that took about 35 minutes to Sao Felipe. One of the pilots was definitely a Cape Verdean, the other pilot seemed to be Portuguese, but in Cape Verde, one really never knows.

Everybody was happy to arrive in Sao Felipe and the pilots politely apologized for the delay. A couple of minutes later the pilots were on their way back to Praia.

Timing was very important in our flight to Fogo. Since there weren't any runway lights, it was essential that we arrived before darkness so the pilots could land properly. The airport was unusually small and what appeared to be a small cottage was actually the terminal processing point. There weren't any other buildings in the airport, not even a tower. I was told that a larger airport was being built nearby.

Several trucks were waiting at the airport to pick up passengers to take them to the village. Since I was traveling with my friend Olavo, I would be able to find a small boarding house for

200$00 escudos for the night. We would have to stay overnight in Sao Felipe so we could catch a boat to Brava the following day.

Olavo asked the boarding house owner if he could give us a room for the night. The owner had a room that was not ready, but he had it cleaned up while we took a shower and then found a small restaurant to go to for dinner.

Olavo warned me that the drinking water might be a problem, so I decided against drinking water and opted for wine. Our meal cost 250$00 escudos and included wine, soup, fish and rice. By this time it seemed that 250$00 escudos was a popular price for meals throughout Cape Verde, irregardless of the quality of the restaurant.

During the evening we had a few cold drinks to quench our thirst and pass the time. I usually drank bottled mineral water and my friend Olavo would order beer. The beer cost 60$00 escudos and the mineral water 70$00 escudos.

The next morning we walked around the village (our boat was scheduled to depart in the afternoon), then I went to the seacoast where the fishermen were fishing and bringing their fish to the village markets for sale. There appeared to be an abundance of tuna caught in the area. Usually young boys would carry the tuna on their heads from the seacoast to the village. they were very skillful in their ability to manage this task without the tuna falling. Everybody had a friendly smile and greeted me with the local greeting, "bon dia."

I managed to walk down a steep slope to get to the seashore. It should be remembered that since the Cape Verde Islands are of volcanic origin, some of the islands are very mountainous with steep cliffs by the sea. Actually, some of the islands are flat and sandy. Nevertheless, Fogo is famous for its large volcano. The name Fogo actually means "fire" or "oven." The huge volcano dominates the landscape of the island and rises to 9,000 feet above sea level. Just about everywhere that you stand on the island, you are at the foot of the volcano.

As I walked down the slope to the seashore, I saw a European family bathing in the sea and playing in the black sand. The sand in Fogo is black, which clearly depicts its volcanic origin. Yet later, I would find that on the island of Sal the sand would be white.

The fishermen had simple rowboats and I saw about a dozen of them on the shore. A few hundred meters away in the sea, there was an old ship that was sinking. It seemed as though it must have been there for a long time. I returned to the village and joined Olavo for a walk around the town and to explore the sights. We tried to get lunch, but the restaurant was not ready. Meals are usually served during scheduled hours in the morning, afternoon and evening.

During our walk around town we met Senhor Monteiro, a popular merchant, who appeared to be in his late 50s or early 60s. He offered some advice on traveling in the area. Senhor Monteiro was the owner of the general store that provided the islanders with a wide variety of goods and services, of particular interest was the variety of cloth used for making clothing.

Finally, we went back to our room and packed up our bags. A truck was already waiting for us (Olavo always had prearranged our itinerary with cab drivers, truck drivers, etc.). We were immediately on our way to the pier where we planned to catch our boat. The truck driver drove past a new hotel, so he stopped for a brief moment so I could view the new building. It took about 10 minutes from town to get to the pier. Senhor Monteiro met us at the pier to say good-bye. Upon realizing that my last name was Balla, he informed me that we were related and that he knew my family.

Transporting water in tire tubes — on island of FOGO

EMBARKING ON A BOAT

Every day I would encounter new surprises. The ferry boat
Furna was sitting in the port about 200 meters from shore and
a rowboat was just off the shore line and resting at about 30
meters out in the water. I couldn't help but wonder how I was
going to board the *Furna*. It didn't take long to figure it out
because a few sea-faring Cape Verdeans asked the passengers
for their luggage and they carried everything out to the rowboat,
which was anchored in water about waist deep. Once the luggage was put on the boat, the seamen started carrying passengers
on their shoulders to the boat.

Of course, when this was done, all the seamen expected a
tip. I gave 50$00 escudos for this service, while Olavo paid out
200$00 escudos because he had several heavy pieces of luggage.
We still had to get to the *Furna*, which was another 200 meters
away. The oarsman rowed the boat out to the *Furna* and as we
were getting ready to disembark, we were told that we had to
pay 100$00 escudos for this service. Well, at least now we were
ready to go; or at least that's what I thought. Now we learned
that another group of passengers were coming, so we would
have to wait for them to arrive. Then, there was still a lot of cargo
to be loaded. In the end we departed at about 4:30 p.m.

The main problem now was that we were all hungry because
we didn't have a chance to eat lunch. We thought the boat would
be leaving much sooner, so we didn't get to eat in our haste.
Now it would be at least an hour or more before we would arrive
on the island of Brava. Fortunately, the trip to Brava was fairly
peaceful, although there weren't any seats on the boat, so
everybody had to either stand or sit on their luggage unless they
were lucky and found something better.

The Captain had a crew of about ten or eleven and everybody
seemed to be fairly efficient. The island of Brava started to
emerge in the distance after about 30 minutes at sea and then I
saw a couple of islets in front of Brava. Gradually, Brava started
to appear, getting bigger and bigger as it seemed like a mountain

rising in the sea. Somehow it felt good to see Brava, because this for me was the final step of a journey that started 47 years ago. Finally, I was seeing for the first time the island that people had spoken about often, but for so many Cape Verdeans in America it was a mythical island that we would probably never see. All this had suddenly changed because now I was only a few minutes away from this mythical island.

THE ARRIVAL IN FURNA (BRAVA)

FURNA - BRAVA

As we approached the harbor of Furna, it was becoming more and more a beautiful sight as this is a natural harbor with a beautiful landscape in the background. The village of Furna is situated directly in the harbor and probably has a population of about 400-500 residents living in quaintly painted white stucco homes cropped closely together. There were many people waiting at the pier as the boat pulled in. There were also several pick-up trucks and a van lined up to transport passengers to their destinations.

I was overcome by the strangeness of my arrival, because I didn't expect to know anybody there on the pier and didn't know exactly what I was supposed to do. Once again, however, my faithful companion, Olavo, came to my rescue and gave me instructions on how to find my aunt's house, since he also knew her. Somehow I managed to jump in one of the trucks and some friends explained to the driver where I was supposed to go. So, finally, I arrived in Nova Sintra at about 6:30 p.m. and still hungry. Nova Sintra, the capital of Brava, is about a 20-minute drive up a mountain road from the harbor.

The truck stopped in front of my aunt's house and I was met at the door by a young lad who was my cousin, but I didn't know it at the time. Then my aunt came and at first it was a little awkward, because although she knew the boat was due today, she probably thought that I didn't make the trip. Since I hadn't met her in person before, this was to be a new experience for both of us. All of my previous contact with my aunt had been through letters as we stayed in touch over the years. In fact, I had started writing her over 17 years ago, when a cousin of mine had given me her address. Yet as the years went by I stopped writing and we lost contact for more than a decade when I realized that it was now or never. Now it suddenly hit me like a lightning bolt. It seemed as though in the past I was always busy and/or preoccupied with other events in life, when one day it dawned on me that I could never rest in peace until I traveled to the mythical island of Brava and meet my aunt. Although I was suddenly committed to making the trip, I was not sure if my aunt was still alive, since many years had passed without any contact. Naturally, it wouldn't be much fun to visit Brava if I didn't have any relatives to see. But, more importantly, I wanted to see my aunt, because my life was destroyed by strife and I did not have any living relatives with whom I was really close. Actually, I lived like an orphan most of my life, but I always remembered the love of my father before he died, while I was still a very young boy.

In effect, it was my hope and dream that my aunt could provide the love that I had known in my father many years ago. Having lost my father over 40 years ago, I would never forget the love that he taught me. Now I realized more than ever that I didn't have any excuses for not making the long-delayed journey. But I still had to know if my aunt was still alive. This means that I would have to write a letter and hope for the best.

After writing a letter from Belgium, where I was residing at the time, I waited anxiously for a return letter from my aunt. Several weeks later I received a reply and I noticed my aunt's handwriting on the envelope. I was in a state of ecstasy as I read the letter; it was obvious that my aunt was in excellent health, despite her age. She was now in her early 80s and she was thrilled to get my letter. Suddenly I felt as if it had been an answer to my prayers. Now I would prepare for the long-awaited journey. My aunt was aging, and she would be the most important person for me to meet now. The stage had been set for what would become an unforgettable journey in time.

These were the thoughts that went through my mind as we met for the first time. I immediately learned that my aunt shared the house with her niece, who was my first cousin and who had several children living with her. My cousin's husband was working in the Algarve in Portugal. She also had some more children who lived in Portugal. I learned that my cousin's father was my father's brother. He was one of three uncles of mine who financed a secret boat trip to the United States of America along with another family of three brothers from the family of Ramos. Unfortunately, the boat left from Brava in 1943, but never made it to America and no one was ever heard from again from that fateful voyage. There were about 50 passengers, including my uncles, Toi, Thomas, and Jose Balla. The boat has become a legend and songs and stories have been written into Cape Verdean folklore in commemoration of the fateful voyage of the *Matilde*, the name of the boat. Many of the islanders still talk about their memories of the disaster as they remember their loved ones who were never heard from again.

Anyway, I was finally at home after a journey of more than 47 years from the date of my birth in Boston, Massachusetts. Now I could see my grandparents' photos for the first time. I could meet my relatives after all these years. I could walk in the village of my father, see life pretty much as he saw it when he left in 1911, seventy-five years ago. Very little has changed. The family home is still here just like it was when my father was born in 1887.

My first ambition was to go to my father's home, where he was raised as a boy. The house that my aunt lived in now actually belonged to a cousin, who let her live in it because it was close to the center of town and in the capital of the island. My father's village is Santa Barbara and is located about one kilometer away and down a steep slope. I would have to wait a while before I could actually see the house and go inside, because my aunt had it locked up when she moved out.

My aunt moved to Nova Sintra when her cousin died and since no one from the immediate family would be able to occupy the house, she decided to live in it. Most of the family lived abroad. The son who inherited the house from his mother was now living in Lisbon. So it was very convenient for my aunt to live in this house, otherwise she would have to walk up a steep slope every time she wanted to come to Nova Sintra. Since in 1986, the year of my visit, she was 82 years old, this was a serious problem, despite her good health. All the necessary things in life were to be found in Nova Sintra, such as grocery stores, medical service, parks and village life in general. Santa Barbara was just a tiny village of a few houses.

Once I had rested and had dinner, my aunt would tell me stories about the family and, little by little, we became better acquainted.

Of course, I would now encounter a new life that I had never really known before, but not entirely unexpected. Even in America we have many stories about the "Old Country." Usually we refer to the Cape Verde Islands as the "Old Country."

Now, I was going to be educated in the Cape Verdean lifestyle. What's a typical bathroom like? How do you get water? Well, I learned that the water had to be carried in a water jug from a nearby well. The bathroom had an old-fashioned bathtub and sink, but it didn't have any water, other than the water in the water jug. The toilet would have to be flushed by pouring a pail of water into the commode. Actually, there was a water tank hooked up to the faucets in the bathtub and sink, but I was told that this would only work if it rained a lot. In effect, the water tank, which was an old oil drum standing upright outside the house under the roof, was designed to capture the rainwater from the gutters on the roof. The oil drum was cut open at the top so the water could pour in. It rarely rains in Cape Verde, so I'm sure that this system was very limited. Nevertheless, nothing really mattered, because I was home and I wanted to cherish the moment.

At dinner time, I would have my first home-cooked meal, which would be another experience. I learned that my cousin, who appeared to be about my age or a little older, would take care of the cooking chores and house cleaning. Meals were cooked on a small gas burner similar to that used by campers when camping in the United States. There was only one burner and all the cooking was done in a small room, pretty much like a pantry in an old American-style home.

Meals usually consisted of fish or chicken and potatoes or rice. Some local fruits were available, such as bananas grown on the islands, but these were very small in size. Bread was of the home-made variety. Meat was scarce, but sometimes goat meat was available. Cow meat was extremely rare.

I learned later that the government was initiating a new program which would be an attempt to breed rabbits on the islands, because of their ability to multiply quickly and provide the populace with a good, nutritious food source.

Drinking water was usually available from a young boy who escorted a donkey around the villages selling water in yellow water cans. I believe that this water is chemically treated and considered safe for the islanders, but I would soon learn that I couldn't drink it. Unfortunately, after drinking the water I developed a good case of diarrhea. It was difficult for me to tell my aunt that I was getting sick from the water and I suspect also from the food that was being recooked without any refrigeration system. The food that wasn't all consumed at one meal, would be saved for the next meal until it was finished. When I became aware of this system, I was afraid to eat anymore.

Gradually, I made my concerns known to my aunt and my cousin. Then I learned that I could purchase bottled water for 100$00 escudos for a liter bottle in a local store. This was very expensive because it was imported from Europe. Beer and soft drinks were also available at about 80$00 escudos for a 12-ounce can. Fortunately, imported items were available on the islands, but usually they seemed to be more expensive in Brava because of the transportation distribution system. It seems that all goods go to Praia first for unloading and then go to Fogo and finally Brava. Naturally, this makes it more expensive because everything is shipped by boat. I found many items to be cheaper in Praia. For example, a bottle of water cost 55$00 escudos in Praia, but 100$00 escudos in Brava.

The first few days in Brava would be confined to the house and learning more about my family history and/or meeting relatives who lived nearby. One cousin owned two stores and imported merchandise from America. He was fortunate to have a telephone because I heard that there may be only about 30 phones on the island, which has about 5,000 residents.

Since my cousin had lived in Rhode Island before, he was used to having a refrigerator, so he also had one in Nova Sintra. In Brava, refrigerators are considered to be a luxury item. If someone could afford a refrigerator, it would usually be a gas-operated one. Such refrigerators could be ordered from Holland or Belgium. The reason they preferred gas-operated refrigerators was because there wasn't much electricity on the islands. This was an acute problem, especially in Brava where electricity was usually available from 7-11 p.m. daily. In Nova Sintra there was one generator that would be turned on just before 7 p.m. and you could always hear the motor running until it went off about 11 p.m. On other islands there may have been more electricity, depending on the island. Nevertheless, electricity was available and one could watch television if they had a TV set. Television was available in some homes because many Cape Verdeans worked in European cities such as Rotterdam and Luxembourg. They were usually allowed to bring in a TV set when they returned to the islands. So, in this manner, families and friends could enjoy television much the same way that Americans did back in the late '40s and early '50s.

A refrigerator could cost about $800 to $1,000 for a small one, because it had to be imported from Europe and then pass through the island's customs and transportation systems. This made it a very expensive item and also a rarity on the islands. I had difficulty in trying to imagine how anyone could ever afford one. Yet some people did have refrigerators.

One woman who owned a refrigerator would sell cold beer and soda, because there was a demand for this service. There was also a bar in the Central Square of Nova Sintra where one could usually buy cold beer and soda without any difficulty. Somehow, most people had adapted to life without refrigerators and TV sets. It seemed that my cousin Bertin had just about everything that one could ask for. He owned a nice home, two stores and three trucks. He was in the process of trying to get approval to build a hotel which was virtually non-existent on the island of Brava. I was told, however, that there was at least one place in Nova Sintra that rented out rooms to travelers and offered a place to eat. Certainly there weren't any hotels available such as those found in Praia or Sao Felipe (Fogo).

NOVA SINTRA

My first real thrill was when one of my cousins showed me my father's birthplace. The old house was still standing and it was probably over 100 years old. My father was born in 1887 and since I was visiting Cape Verde in 1986, it was a pretty safe bet that the house was over 100 years old, because my grandparents had several children before my father and they were probably all raised in the same house. My father was one of 11 children.

The house itself is located in the tiny village of Santa Barbara, which probably has only about 30 houses or less. It overlooks the volcano on the island of Fogo and faces towards the east. At this time we did not go inside the house. My cousin really wanted me to visit the house located just before my father's house, because his sisters were living in this house. He also explained to me that this house belonged to another aunt of mine who was now living in Boston. I also learned that many houses on the island were left by families who emigrated to America and let their families who remained on the island reside in them. Because of the large emigration population from Brava to America, there was little need to construct new homes. Homes were usually given to other family members who stayed behind. Some homes were vacant because of this practice.

I enjoyed the moment of this grand occasion, by just looking over the hill and staring at my father's home. These were moments of deep thought and reflection as I realized that my dream had come true.

Soon I would actually be browsing around, sitting and enjoying myself in my father's house, but for the first couple of days I would just stare at it from the edge of the hillside. This in itself was an incredible experience. It was a magic moment that I did not want to lose.

Once, while looking over the ridge, I felt the earth tremble underneath and I was startled and somewhat scared. Then my cousin glanced at me and laughed and said that was just an earthquake, which happened all the time on Brava. Everybody was used to that, so I was told.

Little by little, I would venture out into the village and meet new people, while frequently meeting more relatives. I never dreamed that I had so many relatives still living in Cape Verde.

Periodically, I would hang out in my cousin Bertin's store, which was also like a small bar where people could get a drink and chatter among friends. The store had the atmosphere of a general store in the old days in America, especially in the Cape Verdean communities of Massachusetts.

The park in the center of Nova Sintra was the main area where people would sit, gather and talk. There were benches in the park and flower gardens that were maintained by a park attendant. The park attendant even watered the flowers with a hose, which had an outlet in the park. This really surprised me, as water is always in short supply. My friend Olavo just laughed when I asked him how anybody could afford to do that.

STREET IN NOVA SINTRA

MY FATHER'S HOUSE

The big day had arrived for me; this would be the day that would take me back in time. This was the day that my aunt would give me the keys to go inside my father's home, where he was born and raised. I started thinking about the year of his birth in 1887, which was just six months short of 100 years ago. What was life like then, I wondered. Well, soon I would be dreaming of those days. Words cannot express my feelings during these moments. I was just happy to be here.

My cousin, who was a teenager, would escort me through the house and we would be joined by one of his sisters, who lived in the house next door. So, on this day, I finally opened the door and walked in as though I was walking back in time; into another century.

The house itself was somewhat modest and typical of the houses of that era. It was basically square in shape with wooden floors and beamed ceilings. The house was made of stucco and had four large rooms. In the back of the house there was an old oven where bread must have been baked a hundred years ago. The oven was made of stone-like bricks. My father, who worked as a baker in America, probably learned his trade right here in this old stony oven.

In the backyard there was little vegetation to be seen. The island was dry and vegetation was scarce. This was a common problem throughout the islands, that is, lack of rainfall.

Back inside the house, there were still some simple furniture pieces. In the dining room there was a blue tablecloth on the dining table. My aunt had actually lived in the house up until a couple of years ago. The house had been well preserved over the years and one could still live in it, if necessary. There were even chickens in the yard, so I guess that my cousins next door must have looked after them.

The most interesting feature of the house was clearly the stone brick oven. Everything else was rather simple, although still interesting. I bowed my head and gave thanks for having had the privilege of being here. It was a dream come true and I had much for which to be thankful.

My aunt also told me of a cyclone that hit the island in 1981 and caused a lot of damage to the house. She also said that the only picture that she had of my father was destroyed during the cyclone. I was saddened by this story because there weren't any photos of my father in her album. I was hoping to see some childhood photos of my father, but there just weren't any.

Well, the time had come for me to lock the door and I spent the last moments just looking around the house as I was leaving. I knew that this would be the only time in my life that I would have the honor of being in my father's house. I know that my father and my grandparents would have been very happy to know that I made this trip. Perhaps they do know. After all, isn't life everlasting? So, I had spent about 30-40 minutes in the house, and these were probably the most precious minutes of my lifetime.

Walking back up the hill to Nova Sintra, I noticed that my feet were hurting me. Then, as I walked around the village, the pain got worse. The next day I took a closer look at my feet and I saw that I had big blisters that were causing the pain. Now I could barely walk and didn't really know what to do. I waited all these years to get here and now after only a couple of days on Brava, I couldn't even walk.

Despite my misery, I was still happy because of the visit to my father's home. Now I was also getting to know my aunt, especially because I couldn't leave the house, since I couldn't walk. My aunt went to the local clinic, which was about 500 meters from the house, to get a male nurse to treat me. I learned later that he was a friend of the family.

Anyway, the nurse came and I was lying in bed. Everybody in the house became concerned about my sore feet and I had a large audience watching the nurse treat me. My aunt, of course, was there, along with several cousins, and then there were three little girls who called my aunt "Mama." These children, whose ages ranged from about three to eight, seemed to be part of the family. Sometimes I think they slept in the house. I really didn't understand the nature of their being there, but this appeared to be their home, just as much as it was for my cousins. It reminded me of what life used to be like on Cape Cod in Massachusetts. Usually in a Cape Verdean community, it was common for children to stay at somebody's house and become an adopted member of the family. My aunt would later tell me stories about others who had grown up in my grandparents home and said that this was common in Cape Verde.

In the meantime, the nurse was treating my blisters by applying some ointment and then he drained the pus and cut off the loose skin. He then applied some medical cream and wrapped a few bandages around the exposed area. My aunt was at my bedside to assist the nurse during this treatment.

I certainly got some relief from this treatment, but I would also suffer a lot more before I left the islands. The day of the nurse's visit was July 8, 1986. The following day the nurse came back to check on me and give me some follow-up treatment. The date was noteworthy, because it was on this day, July 9, 1986, that it rained. I even remember a girl walking under an umbrella. I didn't think that anybody would even have an umbrella since rain was so rare on the islands.

Actually, the Cape Verde Islands are in the Sahel Zone of Africa, which is notorious for its lack of rainfall. It is this area that stretches across western Africa and reaches Ethiopia while leaving death and destruction in its path. This has been an incredible problem for millions of Africans to try and overcome. It is truly a lesson in survival, trying to live on an island that does not have rainfall to nourish its animal life or crops. But on this day in Brava, it rained and everybody was happy. So I, too, was happy, despite the pain. I was also happy because of the affection shown to me by my aunt as she assisted the nurse during my ordeal. This was a very moving experience for me. In fact, the nurse didn't charge me anything for this treatment. He was only interested in my quick recovery. I found that the Cape Verdeans were poor but generous. It seemed so strange, because I thought those days were old-fashioned and all but gone. Certainly it was an unforgettable experience.

THE EARTHQUAKE

The next day I saw another side of Cape Verde that I had never known before. This was a day that would certainly be remembered by everyone on the island of Brava. It was July 10, 1986. This would be the day that I would actually see and feel a real earthquake. I had actually felt many earthquakes in the past, but this one was dramatically different from all the others. This earthquake I would actually see as it happened.

It was in the early afternoon when I heard an explosion and everybody ran into the streets and looked up to the top of the mountain and then a second vicious blast sounded and the top of the mountain just caved in and fell to the valley below in a great cloud of dust. This was truly a scary experience. As I watched the rocks fall, I remembered someone asking me if I was scared. Strange as it may seem, my first comment was, "I thought this happens all the time." My inquisitive friend said, "Yes, we have many earthquakes," but this one was different and scared everybody. Later on, I learned from an elderly gentleman in his 70s, that this was the worst earthquake that he could remember in his lifetime.

I could also remember the reactions of Olavo's wife, as she screamed, "Jesus, save us!" I had never seen a woman or anybody in my lifetime portray such incredible faith in Jesus as that woman on that day in Nova Sintra. Shortly after her screams, the island became quiet again. Strange as it may seem, I had the feeling that Jesus had answered that woman's prayers. It was definitely one of the most frightening experiences of my lifetime.

During this episode, I started to wonder about the civil defense plans for such potential disasters. What could be done to evacuate people from a small island in the middle of nowhere? I learned that there is an emergency phone system in the secretariat's office. This could be used to contact Praia, the capital city, on the island of Santiago. There is usually an ocean-going vessel somewhere within the islands that could be called up for rescue missions. This would be the fastest method of getting help. Of course, planes could also be summoned, but a fast ship would probably be more effective during a natural disaster such as an earthquake.

During the cyclone of 1981, ships had come from San Vincente and Praia to provide emergency assistance to the islanders. So at least I learned that a civil defense system does exist, which was some consolation after the drama that I had witnessed.

This was also the day that a friend was going to come by and pick me up in his truck to show me the rest of the island. He was going to take me on a trip that would take me through the zone where the earth had just fallen from the mountainside during the earthquake. My friend came by the house to pick me up only about 45 minutes after the earthquake. He asked me if I was ready to go with him up the mountain and see the other side. I told him that I really wanted to go, but after what I had just seen, I couldn't go at this time. Actually, this trip would be very important to me, because it would be a tremendous opportunity to learn more about the fateful voyage of the *Matilde*. Unfortunately, I was still trying to calm my nerves after witnessing the earthquake. In my moment of indecision, I asked my friend to come by tomorrow when I hoped to be a little more relaxed. He was very understanding and agreed to come back the next day.

Now I was really scared, because tomorrow I would have to decide if I still wanted to make the trip. Was it really worth it? Especially after such a scary experience. Nevertheless, I knew in my heart that time was running out, so it was now or never.

I had to learn more about the *Matilde*, the boat on which my uncles apparently drowned with 50 other passengers. The port from which they sailed was on the other side of the mountain. This port was used because it was a clandestine operation that did not have the government's approval. It would be easier to go from this port, which is called Faja d'Agua, because there was less security here than in the port of Furna, which is on the eastern side of the islands. Faja d'Agua is on the western side.

Prior to my visit to Cape Verde, Furna was the only port that I had heard of on the island of Brava. Many Cape Verdeans had sailed on the famous schooners to New Bedford, Massachusetts, about 70-75 years ago, while departing from Furna. But now I had to learn more about Faja d'Agua, because of its history and the legend of the *Matilde*.

The next morning would be July 11, 1986, and I would have to get up early to purchase a boat ticket to Praia. My stay in Brava was nearly over and I had to make return travel arrangements which would take me back to the island of Fogo and then on to Praia, where I would have to stay a few days before catching my flight to Sal. I would have to purchase a ticket for the 13th of July to Praia and once again I would have to stop on the island of Fogo, but this time I would continue by boat to Praia. Some travelers would return from Fogo to Praia by plane.

Anyway, I still had a lot to do before I could leave Brava. First of all I had to secure a ticket to Praia. I heard rumors that I should get up early to buy a ticket, because the boats would be full of passengers and supplies. If I couldn't get a ticket, then I would really have a problem, because there wouldn't be any way that I could catch my return flight back to Holland from the island of Sal. Learning to travel around the islands required special skills.

The next day I was up early and went to the ticket agency at 7:30 a.m. and found that ten people were already in line waiting to purchase a ticket. I was really surprised because the office wasn't scheduled to be open until 8:15 a.m. When the office finally opened, I was happy to learn that immigrants have priority for purchasing tickets. I was considered to be an immigrant, since I had an American passport. So I would get priority along with some other immigrants who were returning to America after visiting their families in Brava.

The cost of the ticket was cheap—406$00 escudos, or about $5.00. The boat would be leaving from Furna and stop in Sao Felipe, where we would disembark and spend a few hours before continuing on to Praia.

After having purchased my boat ticket, I went to see my cousin Arlindo, who worked at the general store. He would tell me about other earthquakes and how people were so frightened that they slept in the streets. This was about five years ago, so the memory was still vivid in the minds of the people.

I also learned that a woman who worked in the store was also my cousin and that she had lived in Pawtucket, Rhode Island, before returning to her native land. She was a young woman of about 30 years old and very attractive. She said that she would probably return to the United States within the next six months.

Soon it would be time for me to decide whether or not I wanted to take the trip around the mountain. I realized that this would be my last chance. The last chance to learn more about my family and the history that I had never known. I was left with little choice, so I naturally accepted the invitation to see the other side of the mountain.

THE OTHER SIDE OF THE MOUNTAIN

My friend came by to pick me up for the trip around the mountain. He owned a pickup truck and the trip would become a fascinating experience. My friend Olavo also came by the house on a motorcycle and asked me if I preferred to ride on the back of his bike. He acknowledged that some people didn't like to ride this way up and down the mountain because it might be a little scary. I agreed with him and said that I preferred to go by truck. Olavo was very understanding and didn't seem to mind at all.

Finally, we were on our way up the mountain. As we climbed upward, I would look down at Nova Sintra below and take pictures of the village. The winding roads looked extremely dangerous and didn't always have railings. Fortunately, my friend and driver was very conscientious and an excellent driver.

As we approached the top of the mountain, I saw an unbelievable scene. A woman was walking up a steep slope with a basket on her head. I was getting used to seeing women carrying loads on their heads throughout the island. In fact, I had been accustomed to seeing this phenomenon when I was a child growing up in a Cape Verdean community in southeastern Massachusetts. I never did understand how someone could balance these loads on their heads, because some were obviously very heavy. The strange thing about this particular scene that I was now watching, was the steepness of the slope. There was a small house at the top of the mountain and it appeared to be the woman's home. I wish I could have taken her picture, but I would have needed some powerful camera lens to get a good picture and I only had a standard 35mm camera. I was really amazed at her agility in climbing those steep stairs up the mountain with that heavy load on her head. She looked like she was walking up to heaven amidst the stars.

VILLAGE WOMAN

Along the way we saw the village priest making stops around the mountain. I was told that Padre Henrique was an Italian and the only priest on the island. There were about three or four priests on the island a few years earlier, but now only one remained. Padre Henrique did have one helper who apparently was a monk. The Padre made visits to all the villages on the island.

The most important town after Nova Sintra is Nossa Senhora de Monte, which literally means Our Lady of the Mountain. This town also has a church by the same name and it is at the very top of the mountain, nearly 1,000 meters up. The two main Catholic churches on the island are in Nova Sintra and Nossa Senhora de Monte. There are also some small chapels in other villages like Faja d'Agua, which may be used sparingly. I suppose that a lot depended on the Padre's ability to get around the island. There are also some other churches representing various protestant denominations and located in Nova Sintra. I recall seeing at least two Protestant churches in Nova Sintra, one of which was a Nazarene church.

Well, I got to see Nossa Senhora de Monte, which overlooks the tiny village where the legendary "Sweet Daddy" Grace was born and raised. My aunt always called him Charlie Grace, because that was the name he was known by on the island. Daddy Grace was the legend who started a church in America and became a god-like figure and worshiped by his followers. In the end, when he died in 1959, he left over 25 million dollars to his church. Of course, the IRS had other ideas about who owned the money. Nevertheless, now I could see his birthplace, which was only a tiny village of a few houses near the mountaintop. I often wondered how he was able to attract so many thousands of Afro-Americans to his religious cult.

Once, when I was young, I passed by one of his churches in Boston and I listened to the music as I went by. The musicians were playing some incredibly lively music that had everybody jumping and clapping their hands as they sang religious songs. I was really fascinated by this music and stopped to peep through a window which was painted so that the public could not look inside. Yet there was a small area where the paint was peeling and a passer-by could sneak a look with a little effort.

Somehow, I was seen by one of the ushers in the church and he came to the door and asked me to come inside and join them. At that moment I saw a sight that I would never forget the rest of my life. As he opened the door I saw the worshipers jumping and singing while throwing dollar bills in the air as ushers walked by and picked up the money. It seemed as though everyone was in a frenzy and completely mesmerized by the music and throwing their money away. It seemed like this whole ordeal lasted about three seconds. Although I was still in a state of shock at what I had seen, I quickly realized that this was too much for me. I told the usher "No thanks," and quickly jogged away. I must admit that the music was very exciting and captivating.

Later in life I learned some other stories about Daddy Grace that would really shock me. Not only did I learn that he was from the same island as my father, but then when he died I noticed that he had left some money to several of my relatives in his will. This was a real shock to me, because there were only about 10 or 12 names listed in the newspaper and at least three of them were relatives of mine. I don't remember anybody being named to receive more than $5,000 as the 25 million dollars was left pretty much untouched by the will and was left for the courts and the IRS to resolve.

Unfortunately, since I did not know my family very well, I never had much of a chance to know about Daddy Grace and his relationship to members of my family. I had only read about Daddy Grace's death in the New Bedford *Standard Times*, a popular newspaper in southeastern Massachusetts. This was the first time that I was really aware of a connection between him and my relatives. Daddy Grace had lived in New Bedford, Massachusetts, during his first years in America.

Several years after Daddy Grace had died, I learned from one of my cousins that his brother, Ben Grace, was married to my cousin who lived on Cape Cod. Since it was only a few miles from where I lived, I was able to meet him. I was also told that he inherited $5,000 from his brother's will.

Another cousin told me that he knew Daddy Grace very well because they both grew up in Brava. He also told me that my father, Alfredo Gomes Balla, was a very good friend of Daddy Grace and that it was my father who inspired him to his fortune and his incredible church. Most of Daddy Grace's followers were Afro-Americans living in southern cities throughout the U.S.A.. I was told that my father had been a preacher in the south, but that he did not succeed because of his light complexion and he was trying to attract Afro-Americans. Many Cape Verdeans are light-skinned people while others are dark, with many varieties of light and dark in between.

I had heard stories about my father's ministry before, but I passed them off as being mere rumors without any real foundation. Since my father had died when I was a young lad, I never had the opportunity to discuss stories of this nature. In fact, I only heard about them after my father's death. Now all these rumors had been put to rest because my cousin was very close to both my father and Daddy Grace. So it became very clear that it was my father who helped to get Daddy Grace started on his road to fortune and fame.

These were the thoughts that went through my mind as I stared at the tiny village of Campos, the birthplace of Daddy Grace. It was a strange feeling, knowing that such a legendary figure could come from such a tiny village that seemed to stand still in time, in the middle of the Atlantic Ocean.

Anyway, while I was visiting Nossa Senhora de Monte, I was able to meet a few young men who discussed their hopes and dreams of going to America. One young man of about 21 years of age told me that he was working on the new airport that was being developed near Faja d'Agua and Ponte de Padre. He said that he was earning 115$00 escudos a day (about $1.50) and that a truck picked up the workers and took them to and from work each day. The worksite was about a 30-minute trip at the bottom of the mountain. Apparently they were used to making such a trip on a daily basis, but for some people, such as myself, this would be an adventure. My new acquaintance also reminisced over the previous day's earthquake. He said that everybody was scared to death, especially the people who lived in houses that are on the edge of the mountain. He also echoed a theme that seemed to be prevalent in Brava and probably throughout the islands and that was the dream to go to America one day. This was a common hope among many people, because just about everybody has relatives in America. Although progress is certainly being made in the country, one can't help but wonder about the future prospects for survival. On the other hand, this situation would probably be the case in any country that consists of a few small islands.

While atop the mountain in Nossa Senhora de Monte, I took a picture of the church which bears the same name as the village. Over all, it was an interesting visit and it was obvious that the local villagers were happy to speak with an American.

FAJA d'AGUA

Finally, we descended the mountain and came to Faja d'Agua. Now, for the first time, I saw a beach on the island of Brava and a few people were swimming. There really weren't many places where one could actually swim, because the water was deep and looked a little dangerous for swimming. I suppose it may have been safe close to the shoreline.

When we arrived in Faja d'Agua it seemed to be a village completely separated from the other side of the mountain by rugged mountain roads. It is a small village of about 100 inhabitants. At one end of the village there was a small hotel being built, but I was told that work had been suspended. Nobody seemed to know why the work had stopped except that the developer was away and no one knew much about the project. Someone did say that the hotel was being built because of the airport, which was under construction and only about 2 kilometers away.

Brava did not have an airport like the other islands because it was difficult to find a location suitable to construct one. Somehow it was decided that Faja d'Agua would be the best location for construction of the airport. In spite of this decision, it would still be a difficult job to complete, because of the rugged mountains and hilly terrain. This would require that the land be leveled. Since today was a Saturday, there wasn't any work at the airport so we could walk around and see the development. At this phase of the work, the main project was to level the land and one front end loader was parked at the construction site. There was also a small shack nearby that was probably being used as a tool shed. It was obvious that when the airport was completed it would only be able to accommodate small aircraft. However, this would be all that was really needed to meet the needs of the island.

PONTE DE PADRE

Between the airport construction site and the village of Faja d'Agua, I would find Ponte de Padre, which is a black rocky strip of terrain that juts out into the ocean as if to extend itself into eternity. It is this spot where the hopeful passengers had departed on the fateful voyage of the *Matilde* back in 1943. Now for the first time I could see the spot that became part of the island's folklore, the spot from which the *Matilde* was last seen and the spot from which more than 50 passengers had hoped to reach America, but never made it. This was the spot from which my three uncles had departed on their last voyage, so it was a very significant spot for me. I thought to myself that I was lucky to be born in America, because so many of my family never made it; as well as many others who were lost at sea on that fateful journey.

My aunt would tell me that it was strange that the loss was never reported to any country or by any country. She remembers that it was during a time of war and many vessels were at sea, but there isn't any record of the disappearance of the *Matilde*. My aunt also suggested that her mother (my grandmother) never seemed to recover from this loss and this probably caused her health to deteriorate and she eventually died about 2-1/2 years later.

So, for me, these were silent moments as I just stared out at Ponte de Padre and reflected on history as I learned the secrets of my past. Now I could tell the stories that were mysteries to so many of us for so many years. Suddenly I could see things and understand the meaning of my origins and of the brave men and women who survived the perils of the sea so that I could enjoy the life that I have today. Today there were many reasons to be thankful.

Now I had a sense of belonging to the island and life seemed to have more meaning, because now I had been to Ponte de Padre. This would be the most important phase of my journey after the visit to my father's home and meeting my aunt.

THE CATHOLIC CHURCH OF NOVA SINTRA

The next day was Sunday, the 12th of July, 1986, and I decided to go to the local Catholic church of Nova Sintra, because I certainly had many reasons to be thankful. I suspect that this is the church where my father was baptized as a Catholic. Although he was baptized a Catholic, he supposedly became a Protestant preacher later. But I never discussed this matter with my aunt. Perhaps because I doubted if she could have explained any of this to me. I do not believe that my aunt could have known very much about my father, because he was 16 years older than her and had come to America in 1911, when he was about 24 years old. So my aunt, who spent most of her life on the island, could not have known too much about him, but she certainly remembers him.

Also, on this particular Sunday, I decided to visit the local cemetery, since this would be my last full day to relax in Brava before departing the island. At the cemetery, I could pay a visit to my grandparents' tombstone: Marcelino Gomes Balla and Ana Faria Balla. He died in 1929 and she died in 1945. Strange as it may seem, I did not have many relatives in the cemetery, because most of the family members had emigrated to America or Portugal. In fact, my cousin Belmiro Balla is the only grandchild of my grandparents to be buried in the cemetery of Brava.

An interesting tombstone in the cemetery was the one donated by the Portuguese government to honor one of the island's most memorable poets and songwriters: Eugenio Tavares. I found it to be interesting because of the inscription, which reads:

> Homenagem a memoria do poeta
> Eugenio Tavares—do Governo da
> Colonia de Cabo Verde 1940

CHURCH IN NOVA SINTRA BRAVA

This was the first time that I had seen the word colony (colonia) used in reference to the Cape Verde Islands. Usually the Portuguese government had been careful to use the words "overseas province(s)" when referring to countries that were governed by Portugal, such as Angola, Mozambique, Sao Tome, Principe, Cape Verde, etc. The problem was a very sensitive issue with many citizens of these countries. Portugal had always claimed that these countries were an integral part of Portugal and that the inhabitants had the right to be Portuguese citizens and under these conditions, colonies as such did not exist for Portugal and certainly not in the sense that colonies existed for other European countries.

From a historical perspective, there is understandably a lot of controversy over the issues of citizenship and nationhood. Some historians have noted for example, that although Portugal claimed to give Portuguese citizenship to the inhabitants of the overseas provinces, the vast majority of these people were not Portuguese citizens. However, this is another issue that others may want to explore.

At the conclusion of my visit to the cemetery, I returned to my aunt's house and then went to my friend Olavo's house where I watched television. This was an interesting phase of my visit, because I was able to watch a James Bond movie. Although television was limited to a few hours in the evening, you could hear the news and watch a movie without all the typical commercials that drive people crazy.

I believe that many people who owned television sets purchased them abroad, especially if they worked abroad. Since many people worked in Belgium, Luxembourg and Holland, it was common to see television sets on the islands. Many people still did not have this luxury.

On July 13th, I went to the bank to change some money. The banking system seemed to work extremely well. The bank in Brava was fairly new in 1986, as I believe that it may have been the last bank to be established. The main bank is located in Praia, the capitol city, and the other islands have branch offices. It was common to see Cape Verdeans in the bank cashing checks that they received from their families in America. It was very clear to me that there is a strong bond between the American Cape Verdeans and the Cape Verdeans living on the islands. I believe that it would be extremely difficult for the islanders to survive if they did not receive financial support from their families in America and other countries abroad. Many Americans do not realize how important it is to provide support to their families on the islands. The reality is that Americans should never forget the loved ones who have been left behind.

Finally, I said good-bye to some of my relatives and the most moving experience was saying good-bye to my aunt and my cousin Ondina who helps to take care of her. This was a very sad moment for me and the whole family.

I promised my aunt on that day that I would help her get a new stove to help improve her way of life. I also made a secret promise to myself that I would help support her the rest of her natural life, because I realized for the first time in my life that I had been blessed with plenty and others had so little.

At about 9:00 a.m. I arrived in the port village of Furna for a boat trip to Fogo. The departure time was about 10:30 a.m. Prior to the departure a small group of musicians were playing guitars and singing creole songs. This was a moving experience as people lined up on the pier to say good-bye to their loved ones. At this time I had noticed that there were a couple of foreign news reporters who were also departing the island. It seemed as though they may have been French reporters.

The boat trip would take us to Praia, but not before going to Fogo, which is the closest island to Brava. So we would stop in Fogo for a few hours before continuing the journey back to Praia. The trip from Brava to Fogo was about 1-1/2 hours, so we arrived in Fogo a little after 12:00 p.m., but it would be a couple of hours before we could disembark and go ashore. When disembarking, we paid 100$00 escudos for the small boat to take us to shore. Actually, we paid for a two-way trip to cover the return trip, since we would have to return to the boat after being ashore for a few hours. If we didn't make this arrangement, we would have been charged 60$00 escudos each way.

So while we were ashore on the island of Fogo, we just walked around Sao Felipe and visited friends before returning to port. At about 6:15 p.m. we were back on the boat. During the visit, cargo was loaded on the boat for the trip to Praia. Many farmers would load their products on the boat, which they hoped to sell in the marketplace in Praia. Finally, at 8:15 p.m., the boat was ready to leave for Praia.

The next phase of the trip to Praia would prove to be an adventure. It would be an overnight trip that would take about seven hours. The boat was crowded and there was no place for me to lie down, or even sit down to take a short nap. Some of the passengers were fortunate and found a place to sleep; however, it was not easy, because there were goats and chickens on the boat and some people were getting seasick and vomiting on the boat. Despite the agony of this trip, I would certainly recommend it to anyone who visits Cabo Verde, because it is a remarkable way to experience the mood of the people and the islands. Somehow it gives you a feeling and understanding of a nation's struggle for survival that has endured the last 500 years and continues to this day.

I had the option of taking a plane from Fogo to Praia. In fact, some of the passengers from Brava did this, but I preferred the boat so I could experience the trip. I must admit that it was an unforgettable journey and well worth it. Suddenly you start to appreciate the people around you and share your experiences together.

On July 14th we arrived in Praia on the main island at about 3:00 a.m., but we would not disembark until 7:20 a.m. Now everybody was tired and sleepy and this would be the next problem. When we were on Fogo, my friend Olavo tried to call ahead to Praia and make a hotel reservation, but was unable to do so. On this day there were many travelers and tourists in Praia and, as fate would have it, all the hotels were full. At least one hotel asked me to check back with them later that evening. Naturally, many of the other passengers had friends or relatives who would give them a place to stay if they did not get a hotel room. Others were able to get a room if they got the right hotel at the right time. So my problem would be to spend the day trying to stay awake. I also had to pray that I could get a room, because hotel space was limited. I'm not sure what my options were if I didn't get a room.

I spent most of the day in the central park talking with friends who were returning to Rhode Island after a trip to Brava. Somehow they were talking to a poet and writer who was sitting in the park and writing poetry, so I sat down with the poet and joined in the conversation. The poet, who appeared to be in his 60s and carried a little belly, seemed to be an interesting person. He wore glasses and had a scholarly look about him that intrigued me. Eventually he asked me my name and when I told him my last name was Balla, he looked at me in surprise as he realized that we were cousins. Since there is only one Balla family in all of Cabo Verde, this is a fact of life. Naturally, we started talking about our family history and he explained to me that his mother was from Madeira and lived in Cabo Verde until she died at the age of 107. He also had written poems about his mother. My cousin's name was Antonio Faria de Rosa and he was also returning to Rhode Island, but he had some children who lived in Santa Caterina and he was visiting them for a while. My new cousin would turn out to be a very interesting person, as he knew my aunt Elvira very well and was knowledgeable in family history. I was surprised to learn that although he lived in Rhode Island, he had not yet learned English, so all our conversations were in Portuguese, since I did not know Crioulo very well. It was also interesting for me to learn that my cousin Antonio was one of the rare Cape Verdeans who could read and write Crioulo, the local island language that was spoken by many of the natives on an informal basis. Of course, most of the people speak Portuguese and this is the official language of the school system. Nevertheless, it was very important to know that Crioulo can be written down by writers. Most American Cape Verdeans had only known Crioulo as a spoken language that was never written down. Apparently it is a language mixed between Portuguese and some of the African languages and spoken among Cape Verdeans around the world. It seemed like the Cape Verdean history has been around for centuries, but rarely written down by scholars. Now I was face to face with a Cape Verdean scholar who was equally adept in both Portuguese and Crioulo, this was a rare experience.

I had spoken to Cape Verdean writers in the past and I was told that books are not written in Crioulo because it was too complicated, as each island developed their own dialect; so it was better for everyone if the written language would be Portuguese so everybody would understand it, in addition to the peoples of other Portuguese-speaking countries. I guess it's better this way because it would be a complicated task trying to teach everybody the written Crioulo language, because Cape Verdeans usually speak three languages and read and write two. For example, most Cape Verdeans have to speak and write the language of their adopted country abroad, such as English in America and Canada, or Dutch in Holland; then they usually speak, read and write Portuguese so they are able to communicate with Cape Verdeans and other Portuguese-speaking people around the world. Finally, they learn Crioulo at home as a separate dialect on different islands and when they emigrate to different parts of the world, they bring their different dialects with them. Naturally, many of them settle in settlements which reflect their island background from Cabo Verde. For example, if they emigrated from Brava, then many people from Brava would settle in the same areas in the United States, thus their language would be greatly influenced by their new environment as well as their past environment on Brava. In effect, they would be developing a somewhat different language than perhaps another group who settle in Holland. Yet it's still amazing to know that Cape Verdeans have a lot in common with one another in different countries around the world.

Certainly I was learning more about the history and languages of the Cape Verdean people. I was constantly making new discoveries. My next task for this day was to find a hotel room so I could relax. Fortunately, the receptionist at the hotel decided to give me a room at 7:00 p.m. She was a very friendly person who seemed to be genuinely concerned for my welfare. Somehow I believe that she made an extra effort to make sure that I got a room.

Finally that evening I had dinner at the hotel and went to bed at 9:00 p.m., because I was really tired and in need of sleep. The next day, an elderly man in his seventies, Luis Jose Lopes, assisted me in getting my return plane ticket from Praia to the international airport on the island of Sal, where I would get my connecting South African flight to Rotterdam, Holland. I quickly learned that it was best to use local assistance in getting administrative matters processed, because it could be confusing to the uninitiated. In this regard, my new friend Luis was a blessing. He seemed to spend a lot of time sitting around the hotel and was available to help people in distress. I was still having trouble with my feet, so Luis was able to help me find a nurse to get some medical treatment. I would have to spend the next couple of days in Praia while awaiting my flight to Sal. Fortunately, I felt at home in Praia because I had friends and relatives to see, so I was always busy. Once I purchased the medication to treat my feet, I would spend some time in the hotel just to relax.

Time was very precious to me despite my medical problems, so I would still go to the park and join my cousin Antonio for a friendly conversation and to learn more about my family history.

THE MADEIRA CONNECTION

It became apparent to me that Madeira played an important role in the history of Cabo Verde. Earlier, while I was in Brava, my aunt had told me that my grandparents had come to Cabo Verde from Madeira. She also said that many Madeirans had settled in Brava and Fogo. In the case of my grandfather, Marcelino Gomes Balla, he was a ship's captain who sailed between Madeira and Cabo Verde and probably to Guinea Bissau while in the service of Portugal. So, my cousin Antonio would reinforce this historical data as I learned that his mother was my great aunt. I also learned that he had several children who lived in Holland and France. So I found myself constantly learning more and more about the people of Cabo Verde.

The more we talked, the more it became apparent that some Cape Verdeans had their roots in other countries as well. The Cape Verdean people are truly an international people.

I once recall that when I was growing up in Massachusetts, one of my friends had wondered why we Cape Verdeans were a people of so many different colors, while it seemed that other people were either white or black. Strangely enough, another friend, Donnie Lima, quickly remarked, "God made us that way." We all laughed at that remark, but that was about the only answer that made any sense up until that time, because nobody every knew our true history.

In most Cape Verdean families (with the same mother and father) the children's complexions ranged from near white to very dark. Some had blue eyes, some had green eyes, many had hazel eyes, and the others had brown eyes. The texture of hair in the same families could be very fine and straight, fine and curly, coarse and straight, or coarse and curly. Some even had coarse, kinky hair. So in the public sector, family members were pitted against each other for good positions. If they looked as though they could pass for white, they would get the good jobs that made them visible, otherwise they were doomed for the cranberry bogs and strawberry patches. Early on, these young

Cape Verdeans learned that they had to move out of the Cape Verdean community if they ever completed high school in order to make it in life.

Despite the fact that 17% of the people of Wareham, Massachusetts, were Cape Verdeans, I personally never knew a single person who ever told me the geographical location of Cabo Verde, or could explain our diverse ethnic background. In historical terms, we were always learning about the European immigrants to America and we were even told that Africans had come to America as slaves in chains, but nobody ever told us how we came to America although we represented a significant segment of the local population. In fact, we usually dominated many of the sporting events in Massachusetts, Connecticut, and Rhode Island. I remember some of the oppressions we endured in our childhood in Wareham, Massachusetts. At the time, we had recently moved to the village of Onset, and lived in the Cape Verdean community of the village. There we had a school named the Oak Grove School, which was a grammar school. It was basically a Cape Verdean school in America with Anglo instructors who frequently persecuted the students. I recall an incident in which nearly every student in the class was forced to "stay back" for one school year because the teacher, Mrs. Anderson, was able to discriminate against the students and the Cape Verdean parents were at a loss in trying to deal with such an outright case of discrimination. The details of this incident are somewhat vague, because I was not in the class at the time. I arrived a year after the fact, and could not understand why all of the students in my class (the second grade) were a year older than I was. Once I started asking questions, I was horrified at the answers. Then I learned that almost everyone in the class "stood back" because the teacher did not like crioulos, so she gave them a failing grade. This same teacher was also known to make the Cape Verdean girls comb and braid her hair at her desk in front of the rest of the class. To me, young as I was, this represented the ultimate insult to the Cape Verdean people.

The U.S. school system has dismally failed in the teaching of Cape Verdean history, despite the fact that America is home for the largest Cape Verdean population in the world outside of Cabo Verde.

How well I remember in the second grade, being called on to read a paragraph from a book called, *Little Black Sambo*. It was a story about a little black boy called "Sambo" who ate a ton of pancakes and let a tiger chase him around and around a tree until the tiger melted into butter so "Sambo" could have lots of butter on his pancakes. For years I would not eat pancakes in public, for fear that I would be called "Little Black Sambo." This was the kind of "mental degradation" that was used by the school system in the Cape Verdean community to break a child's spirit in his early years.

So, as I spoke more and more with my cousin, I learned that we have a very diversified and rich culture. Our culture should be explained to the world and certainly to the American people who are completely ignorant of our background and our accomplishments in history. These were the thoughts that passed my mind in my final moments in Cabo Verde. I was getting the feeling that the story of the Cape Verdean people must be told. Cape Verdeans are a courageous people who have been completely ignored by America and many other countries of the world.

So, finally, my trip was coming to an end. The last couple of days were spent mostly talking to my friends and relatives in Praia and enjoying the company of my friend, Luis. Luis fell in love with my western style hat that I had purchased in Belgium for about $35.00. It was only natural that Luis was able to talk me out of my hat, but I had to give him credit, he was a good talker and I gave him the hat as well as a few other things. It seems that we as Americans have a tendency to take our way of life for granted and don't realize the value that others around the world place on our lifestyle. One thing that I realized while in Cabo Verde, is that the hopes of many people are tied directly to the families who live abroad and are able to provide some support to those who still live on the islands.

FINAL MOMENTS IN CABO VERDE

On July 19th, I finally left Praia for Sal, where I would await my flight to Holland. Since I had a few hours to spare, I would just walk around the local village and chat with people and enjoy my final moments on this great and wonderful journey. I bought an ice cream cone of soft vanilla ice cream in one of the local stores. I must admit that it was very tasty and inexpensive as well. I also noticed some little girls watching me eat my ice cream, so it was only natural for me to buy them some, too. Unfortunately, one of the girls dropped her cone, so I had to buy her another, much to my dismay. Nevertheless, I was thankful that I had the opportunity to buy them the ice cream, because it seemed that I wanted to tell somebody that I had much to be thankful for and this was just a small way to show my appreciation for the hospitality that I had enjoyed on the islands.

Later on that day I enjoyed a good meal at one of the local restaurants near the airport and once again the price was 250$00 escudos and the meal was good. Although I didn't know anyone on Sal, I remember my cousin Antonio telling me that I had a cousin who worked as an airline hostess for the Cape Verdean Airlines and lived near the airport. On this particular day I learned from another hostess that my cousin was not working, because she was on her break until the next day. So, sadly for me, I wouldn't get to meet my cousin before leaving Cabo Verde.

Anyway, it was a day to relax and enjoy. I observed construction projects going up in various parts of the local village and especially at the airport where progress was being made on the modernization of the airport. In fact, throughout my visit it was obvious that there were ongoing economic development projects in progress, especially in the construction and agriculture trades. There were many projects that were designed to help increase the vegetation on the islands. This was especially important because of the difficulty of dealing with a terrain of volcanic origin and little rainfall to enrich the soil. Many of these problems were being overcome through irrigation and the use of seawater processed through desalinization plants.

European tourists could already be seen coming to Cabo Verde, but the tourism industry at this time was very limited, because the government was clearly interested in developing an infrastructure to support a tourist industry prior to going all out for tourism. The argument was that the government needs tourism, but logical priorities must be established first. The needs of the people should be met first and this means better housing, healthcare, schools, agriculture, etc. Tourism would be developed as the economy is developed so that the needs of the tourists could be met. So, obviously, this could be a very complex juggling act. Obviously tourism brings in hard currency which is needed to support a fledgling economy.

In order to truly understand the problem, one has to realize that Portugal did very little in the development of the islands. The islands were economically devastated and the land was barren and the people hungry. The nation is now making progress, but it takes time. Fortunately, there are international programs that are helping.

I personally had the impression that although the people of the United States were supporting their families in Cabo Verde, the U.S. government could do a lot more, since the Cape Verdean people have done so much for the United States. It seemed to me at least that other countries were providing much more visible economic aid than the United States and the U.S. Embassy looked insignificant when compared to the Embassy of the Soviet Union. It just didn't seem to make sense to me when one realizes the contributions of Cape Verdean Americans to the U.S. economy. Especially when one thinks of the foreign aid given to Israel and other countries that have a strong lobby in Washington. Hopefully, one day these inequities will be realized by the U.S. government and Cabo Verde will get its just due in the world.

These were my last minute reflections as I departed Cabo Verde. From here I would go to Holland and return to Belgium where I was working. Fortunately, I had a telephone number for my cousin Antonio's daughter, who was married and living in Rotterdam. So, when I arrived at the airport in Holland, I was able to call my cousin LaLa, who would meet me at the train station in Rotterdam. This would certainly be a great way to end a long journey.

LaLa was a very attractive girl in her 30s and had two children, a small boy about 7 and a girl about 6 years old. She was a very friendly person and was happy to meet me. She introduced me to her husband and children and we spent a few hours walking and talking, so as to get to know a little more about our family history. We also took photos as a memory of our new acquaintance. Later she would invite me back for a weekend visit so we could become better acquainted and enjoy the moment.

I certainly had a long and unforgettable journey, so now I would return to the travel agency that had given me so much valuable assistance in making sure that I had a pleasant journey. At the end of my visit with my cousin, she took me to the S.V.K. Travel Agency at Nieuwe Binnenweg 195-3021 G B Rotterdam, telephone: 010-4778662. This is the agency that arranges for the travel of Cape Verdeans in Holland and where one can be assured of friendly, hospitable service. In my case, for example, I was introduced to other travelers who were asked to look out for me so I wouldn't get lost after my arrival in Cabo Verde. In fact, this was how I had met my new friend Olavo, because the travel agency had been trying to find someone who knew my family in Cabo Verde, so my trip would be easier. The biggest problem had been trying to find someone from the island of Brava. The agency told me that there weren't too many people in Rotterdam who were from Brava. It seemed that most of the Cape Verdeans in Rotterdam were from either Sao Vincente or Sao Nicolau. Apparently most of the people from Brava were in New England (especially southeastern Massachusetts and/or Rhode Island).

Naturally, I was happy when I met Olavo, because his wife was a close friend of my aunt in Nova Sintra—Brava. I also enjoyed a new friendship with one of the assistants who worked with the agency. All of the employees made the traveler feel welcome and at home.

When I returned to the agency after my long journey, Mr. Reis, the director, asked me if I had found my family, and I was happy to tell him that I found some of them right here in Rotterdam. I then introduced him to my cousin's family and he was delighted to know that everything worked out well for me. So now I could return to Belgium with the knowledge that I had just gone back a few years in time and discovered who I really was. Now I could tell my own story of Cabo Verde after listening to everybody else for the first half of my life.

When I finally returned to Belgium, I was able to show photos of my journey to my friends in the Cape Verdean communities of Brussels and Antwerp and everybody was excited to know that I had a successful journey. They were also happy to see pictures of the "Old Country," because many of them had not been back for a few years and probably none of them had been to Brava.

EUROPEAN CAPE VERDEANS

At this time I would like to make a few comments about the Cape Verdeans in Europe. Most of the Cape Verdeans settle in large cities such as Rotterdam and Antwerp where one can find restaurants, bars and hotels owned and managed by Cape Verdeans. It's a pleasant surprise for an American Cape Verdean to find Cape Verdean communities throughout Europe, where the feeling of the old country is very much alive, just as it is in New Bedford, MA, or Providence, RI.

There are many Cape Verdean bands that play typical Creole music and they frequently travel between Antwerp, Belgium, and Rotterdam, Holland, which is about a one-hour train trip between the two cities. There are also large Cape Verdean communities in Luxembourg, Italy, and Portugal. Scattered settlements exist in Spain and France. It's usually easy to meet Cape Verdeans because everybody seems to know somebody else in another country. It's one of the most incredible networks of cultural solidarity in the world. This is especially true when one considers how small the nation of Cabo Verde really is. It seems that in order to survive, we have managed to keep our 500-year-old history unbroken, by keeping in touch with friends and relatives around the globe, despite being largely ignored as a people by the United States of America and some other countries.

The Cape Verdean people have lived and struggled as immigrants in foreign lands around the world. Our labor has been used to develop large industries such as fishing and cranberries. It was a Cape Verdean in Paris who was head of the French National Chemical Society and played a major role in the discovery of radium along with Peter and Marie Curie.

Europe is flourishing with the richness of Cape Verdean music and culture. So for anyone who plans on traveling to Europe, I would strongly recommend a visit to Rotterdam and Antwerp in addition to Lisbon. Naturally, there are many Cape

Verdeans living in Lisbon and the surrounding areas, because many Cape Verdeans are natural Portuguese citizens.

ELEMENTS OF THE CAPE VERDEAN DILEMMA

Major elements of the current day Cape Verdean dilemma go back prior to our existence as a people or at a time when we could not possibly control our destiny. The first major disaster was when the Pope, in 1445, published a papal bull which authorized Portugal to reduce all infidels to slavery. This philosophy could be exploited where Christians dominated. Once they (the Africans or infidels) became slaves, the Portuguese had the right to Christianize them.

The second major disaster was a series of papal bulls that divided the world between Spanish conquest and Portuguese conquest in 1493 and 1494. In other words, both of these elements reduced, at first, the Africans to slavery and then the Cape Verdeans to pawns in the service of the Pope and the Portuguese crown. The purpose of this service was to Christianize the Africans and organize the slave trade through Cabo Verde to the "new world." This feature of colonialism was new to the world and had established itself as the basis for the economies of the American countries, even before Columbus sailed to the new world in 1492.

It was this element that would become the model for the rest of Europe after the Europeans reached America. Throughout this ordeal, Cape Verdeans were led to believe that they were Christian, Portuguese, and white. So, in effect, the Catholic Church and the Pope reduced the role of the African to slavery and then used the Cape Verdeans to enforce her rule through the Portuguese kingdom.

The final element and perhaps the most devastating to the Cape Verdean people was the principal of bicameral mind control. Once the Cape Verdeans were born into a situation in which they had practically no control (on the islands and as a new ethnic group) under the leadership of the Portuguese and the church, their minds were effectively controlled to actually believe that they were in fact Portuguese and white, and were serving a higher cause. This worked great, as they must have believed that this was the right thing to do, because it was all they knew. Besides, their beliefs were supported by the authorities in power at the time. In other words, they didn't know of any other way to survive in the world.

Surviving in this way for centuries, the Cape Verdeans actually developed into perhaps the most important segment of the Portuguese Empire. Suddenly it was all over, when slavery was abolished and then colonialism disappeared. So, what now for the Cape Verdeans? It is probably time for all of the people to take a good look at history and understand that our strength is in our unity and we can still make a dramatic comeback, more powerful than ever before.

One classic example of this dilemma is graphically illustrated by a racial problem in Massachusetts that occurred in the 1940s. The Cape Verdeans wanted to be Portuguese and white, so they were given their wish and the school system in Wareham discriminated against them. The Cape Verdeans screamed discrimination, but nobody would listen to their pleas, because, after all, they were now Portuguese and white. How could the whites discriminate against them?

Strange as it may seem, as Cape Verdeans, we generally feel that our society is basically homogeneous. Yet we have always been conscious of the moments when we step out of our society and wonder how we should behave. I can always remember the GIs who were drafted into the Army during the days of racial segregation. Everybody always wondered how could a Cape Verdean survive in a segregated military organization. Cape Verdeans have many horror stories to tell about the degradation of this human abuse. Many Cape Verdean family members and friends were separated into white and black units. To imagine the horrors of such a system, a person need only imagine himself as being in a white unit and his brother being assigned to a black unit on the same military installation.

It is strange to know that Teddy Roosevelt said that "to lose our national heritage would be to diminish us as a people." Yet, the American government not only has attempted to destroy our Cape Verdean heritage, but also the Cape Verdean family, while asking us to fight for "our" country. How do you ask a nation to restore a man's dignity after such disgrace?

Although color was not important before you joined the Army, all of a sudden it is everything. You are now taught that it is good to be white and bad to be black. All of this under the blessing of legal authority. Your behavior undergoes dramatic changes because nobody understands who you are or what you represent. You have been classified by what "others" think you are or should be and you are taught to behave accordingly. Gradually the blacks fight for civil rights and march on Washington. Some whites and hispanics join the effort for equality. Throughout this drama, everybody is at a fever pitch and bills are legislated and passed for equality and benefits for minorities. A major problem is overlooked as some minorities don't have any lobby or spokesperson and everything is viewed as being either *black* or *white*. As the inconsistencies are gradually noted, hispanics request that they be given recognition also and other minorities come forward for recognition, but still no Cape Verdeans.

Perhaps Cape Verdeans were never recognized because in their own minds they were still Portuguese until the 1970s. Even though they were obviously being treated with discrimination, *in their own minds they were still Portuguese and this is what to them was a psychological high* in the face of adversity. Now we should look back on all of this, while there is still time to understand it. We should look around and ask ourselves, "Who are the winners and losers?" We can start with our bank accounts and wonder if it measures up to the whites. How about our jobs? How are we doing overall when compared to the rest of society? Are we at the mercy of others? Why is it so?

If we are a people of great pride, can we afford to let others continue to dominate our lives for their benefit? After more than 500 years of being used and abused as a people, will we deteriorate as a people or will we forge ahead with new energy? If we deteriorate as a people, then trust of our fellow man will disappear. There will be no one to turn to in our time of need. Society is already becoming a division between the haves and the have nots. For those of us who think that we are among the haves, I suggest that we take another look. We'll most likely find that there are many strata above us who can turn their wrath against us, which in turn would reduce us to a have not status. Charles Darwin called it "survival of the fittest."

OUR GREATEST WEAKNESS
AND HOW IT'S DESTROYING US

Our greatest strength as Cape Verdeans is obviously our unity, we should already know this. Our greatest weakness is something far different and more complex. The fact is there is a name for it. It is called "passivity." It is passivity that is destroying us. Our society is like the cement building blocks that are used for the foundations of beautiful homes. If too much sand was used when the cement was being mixed to make the blocks, then no matter how beautiful the home that was built upon that foundation, it will eventually crumble and everything will be destroyed. Our passivity is like having too much sand mixed in those cement blocks. While our unity is the cement mix that has held our social foundation together for centuries, it is this passivity that is the sand that is the element that is destroying our society.

Let me explain my reasoning. T. Bentley Duncan, in his book, *Atlantic Islands*, tells us that the problem is in our past and that we appear to be unaware of it. However, he graphically illustrates the consequences of this passivity. He explains that 17% of the population died of famine in the drought of 1940-41 or about 30,000 people, plus tens of thousands more who were left dangerously undernourished. The reason given was that the colonial government took a passive attitude toward the problem and shrugged it off as just another crisis, "an ineluctable fact of nature for which no one was responsible." Duncan himself was amazed to find that the Cape Verdeans (most of whom were of the darker skin) were passive and did not make any gesture of revolt, while tens of thousands suffered and died. He attributes this passivity to the psychological aspect of the past, which makes the Cape Verdeans believe that they are Portuguese and white and that Portugal treats them all the same, so there isn't anyone to blame when things go wrong. Yet, the darker skinned peoples have clearly suffered the most. Thus official negligence is blamed for at least half the suffering which goes back to the days of exploitation by one race over another.

According to one source, there are statistics to show that during the period 1747 to 1970, there were 58 years of famine and over 250,000 related deaths in some dozen drought periods. The population decreased by 10-40% during such periods. The last such famine and drought period was recorded in the late 1970s.

As Cape Verdeans, we *think* that we are equal to the Portuguese and now the anglos in America. Unfortunately, this is what is called a "psychological dream" that just does not match the statistics of reality. Hopefully everybody will understand this gruesome fact of life. Just like the Portuguese were passive to our needs, the United States government behaves in a similar manner. The fact is clear, *if we do not raise our voice in concert with other Cape Verdeans under a unified banner, we will not be heard.* It is this passivity that has been destroying us for years and why others do not know that we exist. We simply don't tell them because it is more convenient to be passive. Despite this passivity, every Cape Verdean knows inside himself that his suffering and heritage have kept him united with other Cape Verdeans, because this is the basis of our society. Are we going to destroy our own society by being passive? History will give us an answer and I suspect much sooner than we may realize. Therefore, as history prepares to answer this question, we should make every effort to make sure that it is the right answer, while there is still time.

LESSER KNOWN FACTS OF CABO VERDE

Cape Verdeans produced the labor that was used in Cabo Verde for those industries that were successful, but the profits often went to foreigners. The coaling station at Porto Grande is a case in point. Despite its tremendous benefits to the Atlantic shipping trade, few benefits went to the Cape Verdeans themselves, as the profiteers were mostly foreigners. The salt mines at Boa Vista, Sal and Maio are other examples. The salt was extracted by Cape Verdean labor for meager wages, and the salt, which was actually free (because no one paid for it in Cabo Verde), was shipped abroad and the profits went to the sellers. Once again, the Cape Verdean workers did not derive much benefit from their labor.

A whole colony of Jews settled on the islands when they were being persecuted in Portugal during the 16th century. Other Jews from Morocco were added to this colony more than 200 years later. French, English, Dutch, Spanish and Italians were all contributors to the racial mixture of Cabo Verde. Immigrants were also known to have come from the Scandinavian countries and Japan, in addition to Portugal and Africa.

Our diverse ethnicity is not unusual. The Jews, for example, have problems of their own, when it comes to defining who's a Jew. Is this a question of race or religion? Jews, in fact, come in many colors, especially those who live outside the United States. They were probably surprised to learn that when they arrived in Israel after WWII, that they represented different racial groups. Nevertheless, because of their *common suffering* and *heritage*, they found a way to unite themselves into a powerful group and we know the rest of the story. If Cape Verdeans can understand this historic example, then we can still have hope for survival as a united people.

Another fact is that all islands did not develop equally and despite the poverty in general, Praia and Mindelo have probably fared much better than the other areas.

Fogo was the second island to be inhabited (probably in the 1480s) and produced raw cotton and also cotton cloth. This fact may be far more important than we realize. Since cotton was being produced in Cabo Verde, it was an industry that was already in place and functional by the time the English, Spanish, Dutch and French colonized America. So there is no question that the cotton industry in Cabo Verde had to have a direct influence on what would eventually be the major slave industry in the south. This in turn would have a dramatic effect on the Civil War and change the course of American history. Actually, the American colonialists just copied a proven industry that was already in place and working in Cabo Verde. This is, unfortunately, where the industry got its origins; in Cabo Verde with African slaves being used to work the industry. It was this technology that was later transferred to America. This means that, not only did Cabo Verde provide the African labor force for Latin America, but also the system to alter the economic and cultural bases for both Latin America and English Colonial America.

Fogo was usually suffering from isolation in the beginning. That is, isolation from Sao Tiago. The development was slow and sporadic as islanders relied heavily on Praia for basic supplies and foodstuffs. The people in Praia didn't appreciate this responsibility and it caused problems for Fogo. The Dutch, along with the cooperation of Portuguese renegades, attacked Fogo in 1655 and everybody fled the major population areas and the Dutch sacked the island for four days. The residents made pleas to Portugal for more Portuguese settlers. This resulted in a decision by King John IV to order his judges to sentence convicts to exile in Fogo. We have often heard about prisoners being sent to Cabo Verde, but now we know why they came. Convicts came until the end of the 19th century. Ironically, a Brazilian friend of mine has told me that many convicts were also sent to Brazil to settle the country.

The Islands of Brava, Boa Vista, Sal, Maio and Sao Nicolau were first settled by goats and not people. These goats were allowed to roam without control and ate all the vegetation. Goats were being raised in Cabo Verde for shipment to Brazil for the new settlements there. Other supplies and livestock were also being furnished to Brazilian settlements. It is clear from all of this that Cabo Verde played a major role in the origins of Brazilian settlement and development.

Brava was probably settled before 1545 by order of Joao da Fonseca, who was its first proprietor. Brava was considered to be the most Europeanized of the islands (at least up until the 1970s). The early settlers came from Minho, Algarve and Madeira. In 1680, new settlers came from Fogo, after an eruption of the volcano. In 1798 the French attacked Brava in an unsuccessful effort to dislodge the Portuguese influence in the area. Because of Brava's close ties to the United States, an American consul was officially established there in 1816.

Maio was not effectively settled until the early 16th century. Due to the disastrous effects of droughts and because of limited water and grazing land, the livestock and human population has always been rather limited to small numbers. As early as 1643, slave ships from New England traded at Maio. American ships were not always peaceful visitors and one pirate ship from Baltimore sacked the Port of Maio in 1818. Salt from the island was traded for slaves in Africa and for manufactured goods from passing ships.

Sal was first settled by slaves from Boa Vista, but this did not become important until the late 17th century when the demand for salt and livestock had been intensified by coastal slavery in Africa. The airport, which was built by the Italians in 1939, was expanded in 1970 to become the largest in the archipelago and can accommodate the 747 jet. European hotels have been built here by a Belgian/Portuguese firm—DETOSAL, and a French firm—NOVOHOTEL. The airport has become the major source of income for the workers, while tourism is showing improvement.

Sao Nicolau was first settled in the early 16th century with families from Madeira and their slaves from Guinea. Between 1876 and 1917, a seminary trained priests and teachers as it served as the center of scholarly life for the archipelago. All of the other islands can be seen from here on a clear day.

Santa Luzia has had very few inhabitants over the years and has been used mostly for raising livestock. The first inhabitants probably arrived in the late 17th century. However, today it is probably uninhabited. One or two shepherds were known to watch over their goats during the 1970s and early '80s, but that situation is said to have ended a few years ago.

Sao Vicente does not have a regular water supply and this delayed its first settlement. Water was brought in from neighboring Santo Antao and until a desalinization plant in Mindelo became operational in 1972. Mindelo has an excellent harbor facing Santo Antao and it also has about 50,000 inhabitants, which is either the largest city or the second largest behind Praia, depending on which statistics you are reading. An English speculator founded the coaling station in Mindelo in 1851 and most businesses were controlled by the English.

Santo Antao is the second largest island after Sao Tiago and has mountain peaks of 6,493 feet and 5,197 feet. The first settlers came in the early 1500s. Many were families from Madeira. More settlers came in the late 17th century and again in the late 18th century, but these were usually from other islands. Europeans from the Spanish Canary Islands came in 1780 and introduced the cultivation of wheat. Mineral springs exist in many places and the island is considered to be the most picturesque as well as the healthiest. Coffee plants are a cash crop on the island.

Sao Tiago was first settled in 1462 and is the largest island and has the largest population. Praia, the capital city usually competes with Mindelo as a center of urban life and standard of living. The first settlers were Europeans and shortly afterwards, African slaves were introduced to the island, which became the basis for a fusion of the two races and thus the beginning of the Crioulos or the mestizos, which became the dominant racial mixture on the islands. Sao Tiago curiously has both the Portuguese spelling and the Spanish spelling—Santiago—in official usage. No explanation is given for this oddity, but some writers say that the Portuguese spelling is seen mostly in earlier literature while the Spanish version is used mostly today.

Boa Vista was one of the first islands to be discovered, but no serious settlement took place until the 16th century, when it was used for animal grazing. The terrain is relatively low and sandy and has been considered as a location for the development of tourist hotels. There are metallic deposits in the hills that cause compass needles to be pulled astray and this phenomena has deceived many navigators and caused many shipwrecks. Besides that, there are persistent and gusty northwesterly winds combined with a strong current which have contributed to shipwrecks. There were 63 wrecks recorded during a 95 year period from 1842 to 1936. Salt is produced on the island, but only a few thousand people live on it.

The fusion of Portuguese and African cultures has resulted in a coalescence in which African dominance is overwhelming on the ethnic side and Portuguese predominance overwhelming on the intellectual and religious side. Certain writers have had difficulty with this phase of Cape Verdean life, therefore creating a problem in trying to define a Cape Verdean. Who is he? What is his culture? One Cape Verdean writer, Manuel Ferreira, analyzed his conclusions by stating, "Afinal: Africa? Europa? Cabo Verde" ("After all: Africa? Europe? Cape Verde"). We can see from all of this that a Cape Verdean is a result of African and European cultures. More to the point, there is a certain element which makes him unique. For example, the crioulo language has both African and European elements; however, the language is essentially Portuguese in vocabulary, syntax, and grammar, but African in intonation and interior feeling. This is the result of the historical relationship with the West Coast of Africa. Baltasar Lopes, who recently died, had a study of the language published in *Dialecto Crioulo do Cabo Verde* (Lisbon, 1957).

Even the European Cape Verdeans are united in the crioulo language, which represents the soul of the people. In many ways the Europeans act African and the Africans act European. A good example is the following account of an English Captain Crowley, who made several voyages to Cabo Verde as a sea captain. On one such voyage in 1683, he wrote that on the island of Sal there were four officers and one boy, including a mulatto governor, "they are all black, but scorn to be counted anything other than Portuguese, for if any man call them Negroes, they will be very angry, saying that they are white Portuguese."

On the other hand, one European visitor to the islands was appalled to find the whites speaking crioulo, "that horrible language."

On the issue of race itself, it has been said that "white" usually refers to someone of preferred social status and "black" to the poor in the social structure. These classifications may refer to anyone regardless of skin color and were used in certain regions of Sao Tiago.

Certainly there isn't any question that Cape Verdean racial attitudes can confuse typical Americans and Europeans. The islands have obviously been settled by people of many races from all over the world, but exudes a special quality in the fusion of Europeans and Africans which is uniquely Cape Verdean. This quality is clearly seen and felt in the music, language, suffering, cuisine, and general behavior of the people.

Cabo Verde is actually the top part of an underwater mountain range which has caused some people to suggest that it may be a part of the mythical lost continent of *Atlantis*. This may help explain why Cape Verdean culture and history have been lost to the world.

U.S. POLICY AND CAPE VERDEAN RECOGNITION

Once the Cape Verdeans themselves fully understand their past, they will realize that, although their fate has been an accident of history, it is this understanding that will be the key to the direction of Cape Verdeans in the future. Much, of course, will depend on the U.S. government's policy of recognition as a unique people and listed as such on American forms, or elsewhere where their race is classified in the United States.

From island to island, the character of the Cape Verdean will differ, but their attachment to their homeland is universal. So what now for Cape Verdeans? Much of the world owes their economic basis and survival to the efforts of Cape Verdeans. Yet Cape Verdeans are not recognized by the U.S. government as being a minority group. Cape Verdeans are usually at the lower end of the social strata in America and lost in a world where they are virtually non-existent in the view of official U.S. policy. The question is, "who cares?" Well, my friend, the answer is no one unless the Cape Verdeans themselves are willing to stand up and demand recognition.

Cape Verdeans have had a hard life. The struggle for Cape Verdeans began when the first settlers established their colony in 1462. The struggle goes on, but now the strategy must change. We have seen that a major problem has been the way that Cape Verdeans see themselves. The world views them one way, while they see themselves in another way. Now they must try to understand exactly what happened, so they can establish themselves in a new era.

The world is changing, soon most nations will recognize that a major world problem has been the desire of one race to exploit another, while in the process everyone loses. In order for nations to survive today, they must demonstrate a willingness to accept all peoples. In the past, the tendency has been for governments to deal with one another for their own sake and values with little

concern given to the common people who have been traditionally used by the powers that be. Now these common people will
rise in the struggle against ancient systems of exploitation. It is
these systems which have been carried on for centuries and are
very much alive in the minds of Cape Verdeans. Many are still
affected by old systems in which they are exploited by others.
The dream of equality is virtually non-existent for the vast
majority of the world's population.

If Cape Verdeans are unable to reach equality status in
America, then the dream may well vanish, because most nations
don't believe in equality. The truth is that the division of classes
are visible in all social systems throughout the world. The U.S.
may not be fully aware of the example that they are supposed
to be for other nations in the world. Europeans have stated on
numerous occasions that the Civil Rights movement in the states
for the blacks represented a model for them to follow. The
attitude is, that if blacks can gain freedom in America, then
certainly lower classes in other countries should be able to gain
their freedom as well. If freedom fails in America, then the world
may be enslaved by the wealthy.

From the viewpoint of Cape Verdeans, we have a fundamental right to be treated just like any other American. Basically, we
must understand that we are Cape Verdeans and that trying to
assimilate into another ethnic group is absurd. We can certainly
work with others, but it is difficult to behave like them. The
world has been taught to worship whiteness and to deplore
blackness. This attitude has caused many Cape Verdeans to
deceive themselves and become confused, because it defies all
laws of equality. The horrible fact is that Cape Verdeans have
been used as guinea pigs in a human laboratory.

PORTUGUESE FASCISM AND GERMAN FASCISM COMPARED

As unbelievable as it may sound, the Cape Verdean experiment was a human laboratory in which the Portuguese government and the church experimented with the question of race and human suffering in order to create a people that would be obedient in a fascist system. All historians agree that Portugal's government was a fascist one for decades and long after Hitler's collapsed. How could a fascist government be created unless the seeds were already there? Very little has been said about fascism in Portugal because, after all, Portugal was basically neutral during WWII and a member of NATO thereafter. A major difference between Hitler's fascism and Portugal's was the way that business was conducted. In Portugal, racism wasn't stated openly as an official policy as Hitler's policies were openly used against the Jews. Portugal's policies seemed to be tolerable because of the need to use the Cape Verdean as the middleman to hold the empire together. In the process, Cape Verdeans rose to high places in the government. Naturally, this policy became a convenient ploy for the government, because the Portuguese themselves were at a disadvantage in trying to survive in tropical climates and adjusting to the Africans. The Cape Verdeans could do this much easier while being tolerated by both Portugal and Africa in the process.

I would like to point out a key observation that many people may have overlooked. Jews were asked and are still being asked to explain their passivity during the Hitler concentration camps and overall suffering in Nazi Germany. The only logical answer seems that they were psychologically unprepared for such horrors as they became human guinea pigs in scientific experiments for the world. However, once they fully understood what happened to them, they quickly became an extraordinary, powerful nation that has managed to put even the U.S. government under their trance today. This is an excellent example of what I mean when I say that we can learn from our past and use our strengths to greatly improve our society.

The Jews did it because they were openly abused by society. Cape Verdeans have not yet risen to the task, because as a group, many are confused about their treatment. Still we cannot overlook the facts, which are clear; we, as Cape Verdeans, do not enjoy equality in the banks, schools, and job markets. We tend to believe others, that opportunities are there for everybody, and once in a while someone achieves that opportunity and we think that it's true.

THE STRUCTURE OF EQUALITY

Perhaps many of us don't understand that many politicians actually think that we are content with our way of life because we don't seem to be trying to change it. We are just "happy go lucky" in their eyes. The Portuguese, after all, taught us well and now it's convenient for the U.S. government to deal with us passively.

If one really wants to know how equality works, look at it this way. How many homes have mortgages in your neighborhood? Probably most of them. How many businesses have mortgages on them? How many people in your neighborhood have loans in one way or another? Now ask yourself, "Who owns the banks and/or other financial institutions that makes these mortgages and loans possible?" Who makes the regulations that allows these institutions to function. Are these anglos or are they minorities. Our philosophy is equal opportunity for all, but strangely, the statistics are grossly lopsided in favor of non-minorities.

The citizens who preach "a land of equal opportunity for all" are preaching their own philosophy, which means that it is their own interpretation of the facts of life. These are anglos who are in complete control of the system that they have created without our consent and without our input. Once they had created their position, they established themselves within this position in such a manner that it would be extremely difficult to dislodge them. Therefore, while they are secure in their position, they have been able to preach "equal opportunity" for the positions of lesser importance in society, such as a McDonald's employee. If anyone has ever walked into a McDonald's headquarters, they will find that all the decision makers and upper staff level employees are anglos. So when they speak of equality, they are clearly talking about those workers who are selling hamburgers directly to the public. these are the workers who are usually teenagers or elderly citizens who are earning the lowest wages possible in a supposedly "equal opportunity society."

The big winners are those who have structured the system to ensure that they retain an upper level anglo society in control of the big money.

Similar structures are seen in virtually all segments of business and government. In those areas of government where minorities have had some input and success, it was due mainly to increased minority voter registration. These successes have definite limitations due to the structure of the system. This structure requires dependency on a finely tuned regulatory system from the upper levels of government where minorities are non-existent.

Business will even offer support to minorities when they perceive benefits directly related to their interests, such as getting government subsidies or other benefits in return for their generosity.

Society has been so structured that millions of Americans have been effectively eliminated from the American dream and a war exists for the "available crumbs" that are tossed out to those who seek equal opportunity. In this atmosphere, is it any wonder that minorities are extremely limited in their aspirations and specific groups such as Cape Verdeans are practically invisible and voiceless.

Does not the established system plant the seeds that create and nurture the criminal element of society? Is it not this element that is blamed for the evils of society?

I'd like to stress in no uncertain terms that all regulatory institutions are top-heavy in anglos and the same is true for financial institutions, which in turn determine who can purchase a home or business. The same is true of the vast majority of corporations. Who determines who gets a job and at what salary? Under these conditions, we are told that we have equal opportunity and therefore we become passive. Perhaps we feel that we are secure with this knowledge, while we can always try to confirm it later and hope that it's true.

Simply stated, if one person in a hundred achieves success, it doesn't mean that the opportunities are equal for us. Equality is probably ten times better for anglos than Cape Verdeans, while there are still some doors that some people have no hope whatsoever of ever walking through during their lifetime.

I'm hoping that Cape Verdeans will recognize this passivity, much like the Jews did after the war. Don't forget that Cape Verdeans were also slaughtered by the tens of thousands. True, it was due mainly to natural causes, but it is also true that it was due to "official negligence" as well. Besides, if we weren't psychologically raised to be passive in such matters, these atrocities would not have decimated us to the extent that they did.

The human experiment is over for us. Just let us look around ourselves and what do we see? Crack babies, drug addicts, broken homes, unemployment, poverty, social unrest, etc. Let's not kid ourselves by denying that these are the direct results of policies that have divided us as a people and which have kept us in disarray while others walk off with the Money, the Power, and the Glory, Amen!

We can certainly perform at the same levels as anglos. Thanks to Portugal's experiments, we know this is true. Whether it was by design or by accident doesn't matter. The fact is that Cape Verdeans had extraordinary powers and responsibilities when given the opportunities, but strangely, the benefits didn't quite match the efforts.

In Portuguese society, many of the benefits go, in fact, not to the natural Portuguese, but to those citizens whose ancestors came from Sweden, England, and Holland. Chances are these people have fared much better than Cape Verdeans in Portugal.

SURVIVAL OF THE FITTEST

Whether we like it or not, the Darwinian theory of survival of the fittest, surfaces repeatedly in all countries of the world. Whereas some people may interpret these findings to produce evidence of racial superiority of one race over another, others will see that certain historical accidents have given credence to such theories. The truth is that once people recognize how they have been used and abused, they will strive to change their ways to improve their status. This understanding in itself is not enough. One must still be cognizant of the fact that groups can only make progress when they work in harmony with one another of a similar group. In other words, people of a common heritage must understand how to work together for the benefit of that heritage.

There will be many crossovers of these heritage lines and we should understand this as well. For example, not only are we Cape Verdeans, but we are also Americans and have learned certain Americanisms. Surely, there will be times when we experience a common heritage because of our Americanisms. You may have seen this when you were in a foreign country. Americans frequently find something in common about themselves despite their racial differences when they are abroad. A major Americanism that keeps them in touch may just well be their common language which others abroad can not understand as well as the Americans themselves. Believe me, when foreigners see Americans, whether black or white, they usually know that they are Americans, by their dress and mannerisms.

I say these things just to remind us that there are occasions, based on heritage that dictate our status and it can determine how we live or in many cases *if we live.* You will also find that Americans of English and Dutch descent are always proud of their historical origins in addition to their American heritage. Heritage is the backbone that gives us a special quality as a people. We have had it all along, but may never have realized the true potential that we can derive from this opportunity. All great nations remind people of their heritage which in turn helps them to maintain that greatness. So if we can see this clearly, then we will be better prepared for tomorrow.

Look at the successful people of America and you will find that the "old boy network" is still alive and healthy. It works well when you have the assets that control large segments of society and have a common heritage. As I write this, I have learned that a certain golf club has just allowed Blacks to join. Isn't it amazing! Blacks have played golf for years, but they could not join THE clubs. I suspect the reason was, that all clubs are controlled by Anglos who didn't see themselves as having any common heritage with Blacks, at least not "common enough" to be in the same club. Hence, we see an example of the crossover of which I have previously spoken. Sometimes our cultures will cross over and we will tolerate certain developments as time goes by. This will be a natural expansion of our culture and heritage which will be dictated by time and events.

So, all is not lost, but it is important to understand the natural flow of events, that is, that heritage attracts heritage and this in itself can open many doors. A good example is the recent German unification. The most powerful military forces in the history of the world could not separate the desire of the Germans to unify their common heritage. If men of your heritage are on the other side of the door and are *not ashamed* of their heritage, then they will be happy to open the door for you. We saw this in the German example just mentioned.

This in itself does not exclude others, it only makes life more bearable in our time of need. The historical problem has been that Cape Verdeans have lacked such opportunities and therefore we have been effectively pushed out of the mainstream of society.

PRIESTS, PROMISCUITY AND RELIGION

T. Bentley Duncan tells us about a black priest who owned plenty of land near Cidade Velha (Ribeira Grande) on the island of Sao Tiago, and when he died in 1938, he named 68 sons and daughters in his will, but admitted that there were many others he had forgotten. Promiscuity was said to have been rampant among all races and as we have seen, it was also true within the church.

Nelson Eurico Cabral, in his book *Le Moulin est Le Pilon*, France 1980, offers some fascinating insights into the lives of priests, families and the church. Many priests had concubines and fathered many children. This was very common in Cabo Verde. He tells us about the prelate Bishop Vittorino Portuense who was in Praia between 1688 and 1705. The Bishop reportedly would go out into the night and evict the concubines of priests. If they were slaves, he would send them to Brazil. If they were free women, he would assign them to a residence on an island of lesser importance.

The Bishop, who also served as Acting Governor for 22 months, (17 April, 1688 to 28 February, 1690), would also invade the houses of the wealthy during the night and rout slave-girl concubines from their masters' beds When the Governor Diogo Ramirez Esquivel died on 16 September, 1690, the Bishop was prevented from ever serving in a similar capacity (Acting Governor) again. The aldermen and merchants of Ribiera Grande and Praia would not willingly tolerate his authorative rule.

Cabral goes on to explain that the church has always been the biggest land owner in Cabo Verde while enjoying a priviledged position in the political and social life of the islands.

While Duncan has told us about one priest with many children, Cabral expands on this subject and gives many more details, such as the names of some of these children. One such name is Almicar Cabral who graduated from the Institute of Agriculture in Lisbon and became the head of the independence movement which resulted in Cape Verdean Independence in July 1975. Almicar Cabral himself was assasinated in Guinea-Conarky on 20 Jan 73, after returning from a reception with the Polish Ambassador. Several other top Cape Verdean leaders have been named as being sons of priests. Many people will deplore these priestly attitudes, but at least in the end it was the direct result of such attitudes that have given Cape Verdeans their independent nation today.

Marriage was said to be an infrequent ceremony of little importance that imposed almost no limits on sexual conduct. The term twins was supposedly used in Fogo to mean children born on the same day with different mothers, but having the same fathers.

The church also had the power to transfer people from one island to another or send them to far away places such as Brazil. Sometimes we may wonder how the people could adapt to the sociological impact of religion in which promiscuity was tolerated by many and ceremonies were mixed with traditional European rites and African paganism. Despite this attitude, there were certain ceremonies that were taken seriously and one such ceremony was the sacrament of baptism. People usually had babies baptized as soon as possible because the Catholic Church taught them that they could not enter the Kingdom of Heaven should they die before being baptized. Since many babies died due to famine and droughts, this was understandably a serious ceremony in Cabo Verde.

Gradually Cape Verdeans in America will learn the stories that were hushed up for years. We have all been told of stories that were so horrible that parents couldn't tell them to their children in America. I believe that many of these stories will trickle down to us. We might as well brace ourselves for the worst, while making an honest effort to put it all behind us. We must learn to face the truth so that we can finally move ahead and reach out to new hopes and dreams.

FACTS ABOUT STRATEGIC LOCATION

Islands were used to orient nations in their navigation around the world. They confirmed a navigator's location in an unknown world. On old maps, the islands of Madeira, the Azores and the Cape Verde Islands dominate the illustrations to show their importance to the map maker and as a strategic point to assist navigators in finding new continents. In the slave trade, it was Cabo Verde's geographical location that allowed slave traders to manage their business, because the Portuguese and other Europeans could not effectively penetrate the tropical African countries and bargain for slaves. The Europeans were not able to survive the tropics and were frequently overtaken by disease, especially yellow fever and malaria. Because of this problem they would be safer and more secure by going to the islands to practice their trade. In fact, it was so important that Spain captured the settlers and tried to bring the islands under the Spanish Crown in 1476 in their efforts to control the slave trade. The slave trade was the basis of economic strategy for Europeans in the days of empire building.

The location of Cabo Verde retained its strategic importance for centuries and was the communications system for world travelers. This is where ships came to trade and acquire travel provisions as well as perform ship repairs. Eventually Mindelo's port was used to refuel ships with coal, after the invention of the steam engine. Even after the invention of the airplane, the islands were still important as Italy built the airport on Sal to transport goods and people to South America. Today it will still be important for transporting goods to Africa. Once an infrastructure is in order and the islands are able to accommodate tourists with a full range of accommodations and services, many people will want to see the past that helps to explain the slave trade and learn how it all began. In much the same way that Dachau is a tourist attraction in Germany and a reminder of the

Nazi extermination camps, so does Cabo Verde remind the world of the slave trade markets that can still be seen. Hopefully such crimes against humanity will not happen again. Everybody, but particularly Blacks should want to see the past. Of course it will be a lesson for everyone to study, including Europeans and the Catholic Church who made these experiments possible.

One last word on strategic location and that is to say that the actual importance of shipping was diminished somewhat when the port in Las Palmas in the Canary Islands was built with modern standards and also the port in Dakar, Senegal. Both of these ports have cut into the shipping trade that was dominated by Cabo Verde for transatlantic shipping. To give an idea of the importance that Cabo Verde enjoyed, in 1798, more than 200 ships registered in the port of Praia and 74 of them were American.

CAPE VERDEANS AND THE FUTURE

In a free society, distinct ethnic and cultural groups should be recognized as such by the host nation in which they reside. Other ethnic groups should be made aware of others who reside within the same national boundaries and purport to defend the same national causes.

Common sense tells us that if we do not exist in the eyes of the government, then despite our labor, we cannot and will not be given the rights that we have justly earned. For example, in the workplace, if one is black or hispanic, he has a better chance of getting a job, because the employer may want to show that he hired a minority in order to qualify for governmental assistance or to make the government happy for some other reason. However, the employer may refuse the job to a Cape Verdean, because he cannot be classified on job application forms as a minority candidate. I've seen this happen on numerous occasions, so I understand the problem very well. Of course the Cape Verdean candidate may be asked to choose a specific ethnic group, but this only compounds the problem, because if he chooses this route, then he only makes work easier for the government and/or employer and more difficult for the Cape Verdean people, as their existence as a people continues to deteriorate.

Unfortunately, none of these concerns would be necessary if everybody were treated the same. The problem is that, basically due to ignorance of Cape Verdean culture, the Cape Verdean people have been used to sacrifice themselves for the benefit of America and the fantasies that Americans have about minorities and "other peoples."

I would like to point out that Cape Verdeans should remember that they represent an international people scattered around the globe. Whereas they may be treated as a nonexistent people or some "other" minority group in America, they should always remember that they are just one of the masses when traveling around the world, and in Brazil they would probably feel very comfortable, because the people are very similar.

Minorities will make up about 50% of the U.S. population in the next three or four decades. If one looks at the demographic statistics of the world, it will be seen that Anglos are the real minority. To better understand this point, just look at South Africa where a few million people dominate tens of millions, because they want control and power to stay on top rather than live in harmony with their fellow man where all men respect the achievements of one another.

In Latin America, the only non-Caucasian leader was booted out of power by an Anglo government. There are those who will say it was justified and this may be true to some extent, but no one will deny that the actions taken were illegal. This brings up another issue—the rule of law. What does the law have to do with the color of a man's skin? Who makes the law and who is supposed to follow it?

You don't have to be a genius to know that most laws are made by the people in power and in many cases they do not represent the people. Where they might represent some of the people, the chances are very slim that effective leadership and representation can exist, because there is always a higher authority that can easily dismantle any gains that have been made. Simply look at the U.S. Supreme Court and study the ethnic origins of this powerful group. What about their special interests?

Can one expect the rule of law to be uniformly applied to all races? Especially when it is common practice for the wealthy to be treated "different" than the poor. Who are the poor? Why is this so? You'll probably find that in most cases power was taken by force and the weaker peoples were subjugated to the laws of the powerful and they have been discriminated against ever since.

We are always told that we are making progress, so we should wait. Why wait any longer when the people have suffered enough and paid their dues? So for future generations of Cape Verdeans and all other peoples, they should try to live together, recognize the problems, but don't be pushed around by ignorance. All efforts should be made to educate the American people by bringing the history of Cape Verdeans and other ethnic groups to the classroom, children should know that everybody has an equal right to enjoy the pursuit of happiness. They should have a better understanding of others, so that they can better accept one another. In this way all of America will benefit as the *best* man will get the job.

People should be treated as people and not as a commodity for trading and selling as is done with employees by the high rollers who will trade away a loyal employee's job for a price which leaves the employee jobless. Cape Verdeans have traditionally helped one another survive and this philosophy can be a great asset.

Cape Verdeans should learn more about their own history. I have tried to provide some of that history in this book. Maybe others will try to expose our great history and culture to the rest of the American people through the news media, talk shows, classroom lectures in elementary schools and universities, write a book, write plays, poetry, etc. Do whatever it takes to portray the culture and heritage of a great people so one day people of all walks of life will know that Cape Verdeans are in America and have just as much right here as anyone else.

The time is now for all Cape Verdeans to join hands with concerned people of all races to seek unity and understanding. There is absolutely no legitimate reason why we should sacrifice ourselves any longer while everybody gets the credit but the Cape Verdeans.

For example, we fight the wars for our country, but we can't find a decent job because everybody is given preferential treatment by the system. It may be disguised in many ways, but believe me, it's there. The laws are one thing, Justice is another. So, I say to my fellow Cape Verdeans all over the world, seek justice in your deeds, don't be pushed around, we are not guests in this country, we live here just like everybody else. We inherited our rights, don't let anybody take them away because of our complacency. Be firm, but don't be violent or foolish. Use the educational system, get your books and newspapers printed and distributed to governmental agencies, schools, libraries, etc. Educate the public through the media. If the U.S.

government won't finance your projects, then try other countries and their banks. Somebody somewhere may want to see justice done.

In 1990 Congress insists on the Russians giving freedom to the Lithuanians before a "most-favored" trade agreement can be worked out, but nothing is said about the "other" Americans who seek freedom in the U.S.A. The problem is clear: Congress represents special interest groups; they do not represent the people at large. I have been amazed to discover that the American people at large do not agree with the behavior of Congress, but instead feel that they have been victimized by Congress and the Government and do not have any outlets to express their true dissatisfaction.

The United States of America represents a multicultural society of many nations and at this time in history has a golden opportunity to re-think her old racial attitudes. In so doing, hopefully it will be self-evident to see that everybody must listen to the concerns of others in order to build a better world for all peoples.

One does not have to be blind to see that all the major TV networks, radio stations, newspapers, movie industries, banks, savings and loans, corporations, etc., are not owned and/or controlled by minorities. Consequently, these are people who support the politicians, people who make the policies to uphold their own interests at the mutual exclusion of poor whites and all other ethnic groups within this great nation of ours.

Every time the Japanese purchase a major corporation, the politicians scream, but nothing is said when the Europeans purchase similar enterprises. It is time that the American people speak out because we are rapidly approaching the year 1992 and celebrating the 500th year of the discovery of America. It is time for Americans of all races to re-examine our history and policies. In this way we will be better prepared to understand the problems that other nations are facing as a result of recent changes in ideology around the world.

If we are unable to understand the problems and make an honest effort to resolve the issues, we will be headed for the "Dark Ages" of history and if there are any winners, they will probably be the Japanese and a few other Asian nations.

To help clarify the point, it is a good idea to glance at a few problems. For example, the United States has constantly bashed the Mexicans for their Third World Debt crisis of $90 billion, but little if anything is said about the $500-600 billion savings and loan bailout. The Russians admit that communism has failed and now they want to restructure (perestroika) society and get on with their lives, while the U.S.A. is singing high praises for democracy and saying, "We won! We won!" Yet if one is willing to open his eyes as he walks down the streets of America, he will see millions of losers who do not have any representation, saying, "We won! We won!"

It is for this reason that I say to all Americans that you should recognize the Cape Verdeans who have struggled to survive in this country, only to be virtually ignored and deprived of their national identity. As a result, many people lose their self-esteem so at first they are the victims of a strange society that they do not understand, then they become the criminals of the society and the circle continues among the downtrodden peoples of this country. So the rich get richer and the poor get poorer. Unfortunately for the rich, the poor people will eventually figure this mess out and the wealth of the rich will crumble and more and more crime is generated because of the attitudes of the wealthy policy makers who have traditionally ignored the "true needs" of others.

I strongly urge the United States of America to review her policies as they pertain to all citizens and then to restructure these policies based on the desires of "all" the people. Obviously in the case of the Cape Verdean population of America, nobody really knows what we want because no one seems to know that we exist.

A classic example was my attempt to get a drivers license in Texas in 1989. When I applied for a license I was told in no uncertain terms that I could be only white or black, nothing else would suffice and the computers were rigged accordingly. I explained that I was not going to be humiliated any longer in this country and that I was prepared to go to the Supreme Court if necessary for a ruling on my case. After all efforts to convince the powers that be had failed, I had to see the area manager in El Paso. Although he was an honorable person, he was confused about the matter so he contacted the state vehicle registration office in Austin for advice.

In the end I was allowed to request a drivers license, after a bitter two week struggle, an exception was granted in my case. I cite this problem only because, as usual, no one knows that Cape Verdeans exist in America. This situation has troubled Cape Verdeans in this country their entire lives and now it's time that we do something about it. We cannot afford to be humiliated any longer.

In the future, I foresee a need for a political party that truly represents the deprived peoples of this great nation, such a party would be fully representative of Cape Verdeans, Hispanics, Blacks, Asians, Indians, Arabs, and poor whites. Such a party would have a much better chance in dealing with most countries of the world. It is only logical that if Arab nations saw that Arabs were well treated in America and "fully" represented in all walks of life, they would have much more respect in their dealings and treatment of all Americans. The same would hold true of all great nations. Americans should reexamine the way others see them around the world.

The Japanese are a great people because of their willingness to help each other; the same holds true for other peoples, but in the American marketplace, we are seeing more and more distrust among the nation's citizens and I believe that it is this distrust that is destroying our nation. Hopefully, there are responsible citizens in this country who will get the country working together so that we can celebrate 1992 with a new hope and direction.

In the America of the future, citizens can describe themselves as being members of the human race or simply as an American or a as a foreigner without regard to skin color. Many Americans do not realize that other countries are usually disgusted with American racial policies and can't understand why color is so important on government forms. Perhaps one day other nations will place sanctions on the U.S.A. until these racial policies have been significantly improved.

Who would have guessed a year ago that the Lithuanians would have a better chance for self-determination than the Cape Verdeans in America, as well as many other groups in America.

In the meantime, the Cape Verdeans of today and tomorrow should develop agencies for the purpose of supporting one another. Such agencies should seek out creative ways to interact between the U.S. government and state and local governments with the specific objective of promoting Cape Verdean culture and history. In addition, such agencies should seek all possible means to improve the job market for Cape Verdeans. Special emphasis should be placed on networking activities to either find jobs for Cape Verdeans and/or assist them in establishing their own business whenever practical.

All such activities should be closely coordinated with active agencies around the world, including Cape Verdean Embassies and Consulates, in addition to foreign banks and/or the Bank of Cape Verde whenever possible.

A special skills data bank should be created by a central agency. Such a bank should be available to Cape Verdeans around the world. The names of lawyers, doctors, business experts, teachers, translators, CPAs, politicians, writers, etc., would be consolidated with pertinent background information. In this way, Cape Verdeans could deal with others who could better understand their needs and grievances. This system could easily bring hope to thousands who are determined to pursue their dreams.

In the final analysis, Cape Verdeans should interact with all people of good will regardless of their ethnic or religious backgrounds. However, it is imperative that others understand that we exist in America and that we also have needs.

THE BITTER TRUTH

How do we put events into reality? We are frequently told one thing but see another quite different. How are we supposed to know what to believe? A classic example follows: let us look at three letters from California politicians, which clearly profess a special pride for Cape Verdean Americans and indicate that they recognize the existence of Cape Verdeans in America. Now, let's look at a California state job application and try to find Cape Verdeans listed as an ethnic group. What we find is a shocking insult to the Cape Verdean people. There are 22 ethnic designations, but none for Cape Verdeans.

If we analyze this matter, we now know that at least three California politicians supposedly recognize our existence as a special people with pride, but in their own state we do not exist on a job form. Is this how we are recognized or is this a double standard? Perhaps the politicians know something about us, but certainly they don't know our true psychological makeup and historical pride. In other words, they probably think that we are content with the status quo. If this is true, then this is one more reason why we must speak out now. All Americans must know that we *are not* content with this situation. *This is why we as Cape Verdeans must learn about our own history so that we can educate the politicians about our true character and pride.*

We can't really blame the politicians for our problem in this case, as much as ourselves. If we are confused about our history, then others will be also. We are probably giving the wrong signals to them without realizing it. I doubt seriously if the average politician knows anything about our heritage. Those that know anything at all, would only have a limited knowledge of our history, because the subject matter itself has been very limited (especially before this book was written). That's why it is so important that we reconstruct our own history while it is still possible.

Congressional Record

United States
of America

PROCEEDINGS AND DEBATES OF THE *101ˢᵗ* CONGRESS, SECOND SESSION

Vol. 136   WASHINGTON, THURSDAY, MAY 17, 1990   No. 63

House of Representatives

Honoring Cape Verdean Independence

Hon. HOWARD L. BERMAN
of California

MR. SPEAKER: It is an honor and pleasure to rise today and pay tribute to the Republic of Cape Verde and Cape Verdeans throughout the world. July 5, 1990 marks the 15th anniversary of this proud country's independence from Portugal and it will be celebrated by Cape Verdeans worldwide.

After an almost 20-year struggle for improved economic, social and political conditions, on July 5, 1975, under the leadership of revolutionary Amilcar Cabral, the Republic of Cape Verde emerged a country with strong economic aspirations and a commitment to the continuance of a fair and equitable society.

Located approximately 385 miles off the west African coast, this 10 island archipelago is developing into a key center for regional and international investment. The country's monetary and fiscal policies have made this young nation a showcase for the World Bank and the International Monetary Fund. Cape Verde's GNP has doubled since independence and it currently boasts an average annual growth rate of 4%. The country is becoming a significant resource for its neighbors and is an innovative partner in regional development.

Cape Verdeans take extreme pride in Cape Verdean Ambassador Jose Fernandes Luis Lopes, the first African ever to attain the distinguished position of Head of the Diplomatic Corps in Washington.

The official language of Cape Verde is Portuguese, but most of the population speak a Crioulo dialect. The rich Crioulo musical and poetic tradition is filled with old fashioned stories of love, exotic journeys and family.

In the mid-19th century, Cape Verdeans were renowned for being a great seafaring people, skilled in whaling and craftsmanship in the repair of ships. As a result, many Cape Verdeans eventually settled in different parts of the world. Of the more than 3 million people of Cape Verdean ancestry worldwide, over 400,000 live in the United States. I take special pride in the achievements of Cape Verdean Americans in my district particularly since one of my own staff assistants -- Margaret Mott -- is an active and enthusiastic organizer among Californian Cape Verdean Americans.

MR. SPEAKER: It is with great pleasure that I ask my colleagues, who have many Cape Verdean Americans in their respective congressional districts, to join me in saluting the Republic of Cape Verde on this auspicious occasion.

1990

SACRAMENTO OFFICE
STATE CAPITOL ROOM 4040
SACRAMENTO CA 95814
916/445-5209

JIM LOTT
CHIEF OF STAFF

DISTRICT OFFICE
4401 CRENSHAW BLVD
SUITE 300
LOS ANGELES CA 90043
(213) 295-6655

California State Senate

DIANE E. WATSON, Ph.D
TWENTY-EIGHTH SENATORIAL DISTRICT

CHAIRPERSON

Senate Committee on Health and Human Services

July 27, 1990

CAPE VERDEANS OF SOUTHERN CALIFORNIA

G R E E T I N G S

Special Congratulations to the **Cape Verdeans of Southern California, Cape Verdean West Association** and **Capitol Cape Verdeans** for their join efforts in hosting the fifteenth Independence Celebration for the Republic of Cape Verde from July 27 to July 29, 1990.

The Republic of Cape Verde, in its short fifteen years of independence, has made an indelible mark on history. President Aristedes Pereira of Cape Verde is a widely respected African Leader and has maintained an open door policy toward all countries in futherance of the economic development and survival of Cape Verde and its people.

Cape Verdean Americans will be coming to Long Beach from all over the United States and from the Republic of Cape Verde to celebrate their pride in their homeland.

I salute you all and wish you many years of continued prosperity upon the occasion of this significant anniversary in your nation's history.

Most sincerely,

Diane E. Watson, Ph.D.
STATE SENATOR

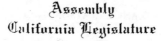

Assembly
California Legislature

CURTIS R. TUCKER, JR.
ASSEMBLYMAN, FIFTIETH DISTRICT

COMMITTEES
AGING AND LONG TERM CARE
HUMAN SERVICES
LABOR AND EMPLOYMENT
PUBLIC EMPLOYEES
RETIREMENT AND
SOCIAL SECURITY
REVENUE AND TAXATION
SELECT COMMITTEES
ASSISTANCE TO VICTIMS
OF SEXUAL ASSAULT
UNLICENSED CONTRACTORS
JOINT COMMITTEE
ORGANIZED CRIME AND
GANG VIOLENCE

June 15, 1990

Cape Verdeans of Southern California
P.O. Box 8178
Los Angeles, CA 90008

Dear Friends:

Congratulations to the Cape Verdeans of Southern California, Cape Verdean West Association and Capitol Cape Verdeans for their joint efforts in hosting the 15th Independence Celebration for the Republic of Cape Verde.

The Republic of Cape Verde in its 15 years of independence has made an indelible mark in history. You can be proud of the fact that President Aristedes Pereira, Ministers and other Cape Verdean officials have and continue to strive to include all factions of society in the political system.

I am delighted to participate in this momentous occasion with the Cape Verdean Americans who will be coming from all over the United States and from the Republic of Cape Verde to share in this pride with their homeland.

Sincerely,

CURTIS R. TUCKER, JR.
Assemblyman, 50th District

1990

EXAMINATION APPLICATION

9987607

PLEASE PRINT OR TYPE

Discrimination on the basis of race, color, creed, national origin, ancestry, sex, marital status, disability, religious or political affiliation, age or sexual orientation is prohibited.

	DO NOT WRITE IN THIS SPACE

1. ENTER BELOW THE EXACT TITLES OF THE EXAMINATIONS IN PROGRESS FOR WHICH YOU ARE APPLYING AND CHECK EITHER OPEN, PROMOTIONAL OR BOTH. LIST ONLY TITLE ON THE APPLICATION ON PRIOR TO NOMINATION OF THE EXAMINATION. [ ] OPEN [ ] PROM

FOR OPEN EXAMINATIONS ENTER THE LOCATION WHERE YOU WISH TO WORK

CLASSES		
WC FOR SERIES		
RECPLAG FOR SERIES		
FLAGS		

DO NOT WRITE IN THIS SPACE

01	02	03	04	05	06	07	08	09	10

WC

2. FOR ALL APPLICANTS
   A. ENTER LOCATION OR ZIP CODE NUMBER (SEE BACK OF ATTACHED FLAP FOR CODES) FOR THE ONE LOCATION WHERE YOU PREFER TO HAVE THE EXAMINATION.

   B. DO YOU HAVE A DISABILITY IMPAIRMENT FOR WHICH YOU MAY NEED ASSISTANCE DURING A WRITTEN OR ORAL TEST? IF YES YOU WILL BE CONTACTED FOR EACH. [ ] YES [ ] NO

   MAKE SPECIFIC ARRANGEMENTS

   C. PLEASE INDICATE IF YOUR RELIGIOUS BELIEFS PREVENT YOU FROM TAKING AN EXAMINATION ON SATURDAY [ ] YES [ ] NO

   D. IN ADDITION TO ENGLISH, I POSSESS
   [ ] SPANISH [ ] AMERICAN STANDARD SIGN LANGUAGE [ ] VERBAL [ ] WRITTEN FLUENCY IN
   [ ] JAPANESE [ ] BRAILLE [ ] CHINESE-CANTONESE DIALECT
   [ ] VIETNAMESE [ ] PORTUGUESE [ ] CHINESE-MANDARIN DIALECT
   [ ] KOREAN [ ] ILIANO-TAGALOG DIALECT [ ] OTHER LANGUAGES/DIALECTS

   E. WERE YOU EVER DISCHARGED REJECTED DURING PROBATION OR HAVE YOU EVER BEEN REQUESTED TO RESIGN OR RESIGNED UNDER UNFAVORABLE CIRCUMSTANCES FROM ANY EMPLOYMENT? YOU MAY OMIT ANY RECENT OCCURRING OVER 5 YEARS AGO EXCEPT A DISCHARGE, DISMISSAL OR A PROBATIONARY PERIOD REJECTION FROM CALIFORNIA STATE CIVIL SERVICE. IF YES GIVE DETAILS IN #10 [ ] YES [ ] NO

   (INDIVIDUALS DISMISSED FROM CALIFORNIA STATE EMPLOYMENT BY ADVERSE ACTION OR DISCIPLINARY PROCEEDINGS MUST OBTAIN THE CONSENT OF THE EXECUTIVE OFFICER OF THE STATE PERSONNEL BOARD BEFORE TAKING A CIVIL SERVICE EXAMINATION.)

3. FOR TYPING OR STENOGRAPHIC APPLICANTS ONLY
   A. I CERTIFY THAT I CAN TYPE AT A SPEED OF [ ] 40 [ ] 50 [ ] 55 WORDS PER MINUTE OR MORE
   B. I HAVE A VALID STATE OF CALIFORNIA CERTIFICATE FOR (CHECK LEVEL) [ ] STENO [ ] SR [ ] LEGAL [ ] SR LEGAL

4. FOR PROMOTIONAL APPLICANTS ONLY
   ARE YOU NOW EMPLOYED BY THE STATE OF CALIFORNIA? [ ] YES DEPARTMENT _____ SUBDIVISION _____ [ ] NO
   MY ELIGIBILITY FOR EXAMINATION IS BASED ON

   C. LIST ANY JURISDICTIONS FOR THE LAST FIVE YEARS (CURRENT SUPERVISOR FIRST) ADDITIONAL NAMES IN #10 IF AN EMPLOYEE EVALUATION REPORT IS USED YOU MAY NOMINATE ONE OF THESE SUPERVISORS TO PREPARE YOUR REPORT BY PLACING AN ASTERISK (*) NEXT TO THE NAME.

FROM	TO	NAME	TITLE	DEPARTMENT UNIT

5. FOR OPEN, NONPROMOTIONAL EXAM APPLICANTS ONLY
   DO YOU QUALIFY FOR CAREER CREDITS AS DESCRIBED IN THE ANNOUNCEMENT FOR THE EXAMINATION? [ ] YES [ ] NO

DO NOT WRITE IN THIS SPACE

5. SOCIAL SECURITY ACCOUNT NUMBER
   (See Privacy Statement on reverse of application flap)

NAME (LAST) (FIRST) (MI/MM)

ADDRESS (NUMBER) (STREET)

CITY COUNTY STATE ZIP CODE

TELEPHONE (Business) (Home)

7. PLEASE ANSWER ONLY IF THE ANNOUNCEMENT FOR THE EXAMINATION FOR WHICH YOU ARE APPLYING HAS A MINIMUM AND OR MAXIMUM AGE LIMITATION (MO/DAY/YEAR)

BIRTHDATE

8. PLEASE ANSWER ONLY IF THE ANNOUNCEMENT FOR THE EXAMINATION FOR WHICH YOU ARE APPLYING HAS INDICATED THAT DRIVING IS REQUIRED UNDER THE MINIMUM QUALIFICATIONS

   A. HAVE YOU EVER HAD YOUR DRIVER'S LICENSE REVOKED OR HAS IT YOUR DRIVER'S LICENSE EVER BEEN SUSPENDED OR REVOKED? [ ] YES [ ] NO
   IF YOUR ANSWER IS YES, LIST ALL OFFENSES IN ITEM #10 GIVING DATE, LOCATION, NATURE, AND DISPOSITION FOR EACH

   B. DO YOU POSSESS A VALID CALIFORNIA DRIVER'S LICENSE? [ ] YES [ ] NO
   IF "YES", ENTER YOUR DRIVER'S LICENSE NUMBER
   CIRCLE CLASS 1   2   3   4

9. PLEASE ANSWER ONLY IF THE ANNOUNCEMENT FOR THE EXAMINATION FOR WHICH YOU ARE APPLYING INDICATES THAT IT IS FOR A PEACE OFFICER DESIGNATION
   A. ARE YOU A CITIZEN OF THE UNITED STATES? [ ] YES [ ] NO
   B. HAVE YOU EVER BEEN CONVICTED BY ANY COURT OF A FELONY? [ ] YES [ ] NO
   NOTE: YOU MAY ANSWER "NO" IF THE CONVICTION IS SPECIFIED IN HEALTH AND SAFETY CODE SECTION 11361.5, WHICH SECTION PERTAINS TO VARIOUS MARIJUANA OFFENSES OR IF THE CONVICTION WAS UNDER HEALTH AND SAFETY CODE VIOLATION 11357 OR ITS SUCCESSOR 11366 WHEN THAT CONVICTION WAS STIPULATED OR DESIGNATED TO BE A LESSER INCLUDED OFFENSE OF THE POSSESSION OF MARIJUANA.
   C. HAVE YOU OTHERWISE DISQUALIFIED BY LAW FROM BEING EMPLOYED AS A PEACE OFFICER? [ ] YES [ ] NO
   (SEE EXAMINATION ANNOUNCEMENT FOR DETAILS AND THE CIRCUMSTANCES UNDER WHICH YOU MAY ANSWER "NO" TO ITEM 9B OR 9C)

10.

11. CERTIFICATION OF APPLICANT—READ CAREFULLY BEFORE SIGNING
    I Hereby Certify, That all statements made in this application are true and complete. I also understand that if I do not have legal minimum qualifications for this class, I will be removed from the examination when this fact is determined.

    SIGNATURE _____ DATE _____

▲

9987607

EQUAL EMPLOYMENT OPPORTUNITY

TO ASSIST THE STATE OF CALIFORNIA IN ITS COMMITMENT TO EQUAL EMPLOYMENT OPPORTUNITY AND IN ACCORDANCE WITH APPLICABLE LAWS, YOU ARE ASKED TO VOLUNTARILY PROVIDE THE INFORMATION REQUESTED. THIS SECTION WILL BE SEPARATED FROM THE APPLICATION PRIOR TO NOMINATION OF THE EXAMINATION. IF YOU ARE CALLED IN FOR A HIRING INTERVIEW PLEASE REMOVE THIS SECTION OF THE APPLICATION PRIOR TO THE INTERVIEW

[ ] MALE [ ] FEMALE

YOUR AGE GROUP
1 [ ] UNDER 21   3 [ ] 30-39   5 [ ] 50-59   7 [ ] 70 AND OVER
2 [ ] 21-29   4 [ ] 40-49   6 [ ] 60-69

PLEASE CHECK THE ONE BOX WHICH BEST DESCRIBES YOUR RACE ETHNICITY

IF HISPANIC, CHECK (HISPANIC DOES NOT INCLUDE PERSONS OF PORTUGUESE OR BRAZILIAN ORIGIN OR PERSONS WHO REQUIRED A SEPARATE SURNAME)
A [ ] MEXICAN, MEXICAN-AMERICAN, CHICANO   C [ ] CUBAN
B [ ] PUERTO RICAN   D [ ] ANY OTHER SPANISH/ HISPANIC (Specify) _____

IF NOT HISPANIC CHOOSE ONE OF THE FOLLOWING
E [ ] WHITE   G [ ] BLACK   H [ ] FILIPINO
F [ ] AMERICAN INDIAN CHECK (Number of your American Indian Tribe or band recognized by the Bureau of Indian Affairs or has a valid document of your blood quantum from tribes or bands indigenous to the United States or Canada.) SPECIFY: [ ] require an identification of American ancestry at time of employment

N [ ] AMERICAN INDIAN (Specify) _____   O [ ] ALEUT
N [ ] ESKIMO   Q [ ] ALEUT
K [ ] ASIAN, CHECK
K [ ] KOREAN   M [ ] ASIAN INDIAN   J [ ] CHINESE
U [ ] VIETNAMESE   S [ ] JAPANESE   S [ ] OTHER ASIAN (Specify)
U [ ] CAMBODIAN   V [ ] LAOTIAN
P [ ] PACIFIC ISLANDER CHECK
P [ ] SAMOAN   Q [ ] GUAMANIAN-CHAMORRO
X [ ] OTHER PACIFIC ISLANDER (Specify)
X [ ] OTHER NOT LISTED (Specify) _____

CHECK ANY OF THE FOLLOWING WHICH APPLY
ARE YOU DISABLED? (A PERSON WITH A DISABILITY IS ONE WHO HAS A PHYSICAL OR MENTAL IMPAIRMENT WHICH LIMITS ONE OR MORE LIFE ACTIVITIES, SUCH AS CARING FOR ONE'S SELF, PERFORMING MANUAL TASKS, WALKING, SEEING, HEARING, SPEAKING, BREATHING, LEARNING, AND HOLDING GAINFUL EMPLOYMENT)

A [ ] HIT   M [ ] NEUROLOGICAL   U [ ] RESPIRATORY
B [ ] HEARING   DYSLEXIA   V [ ] MENTAL
C [ ] SPEECH   N [ ] DIGESTIVE   EMOTIONAL
D [ ] ORTHOPEDIC   O [ ] KIDNEY   ALCOHOLISM
   AMPUTATIONS   P [ ] DIABETES   V [ ] DRUG
H [ ] EPILEPSY   Q [ ] HEART,   ADDICTION
   R [ ] CANCER   W [ ] OTHER (Specify)
   L [ ] BLOOD   S [ ] SKIN   X [ ] NO DISABILITY
   CONDITIONS

ARE YOU A VETERAN, SPOUSE OF A 100% DISABLED VETERAN OR A WIDOW (OR WIDOWER) OF A VETERAN?*
[ ] YES [ ] NO

*Only the names of those applicants who check "yes" will be verified for veterans preference points in examinations which allow the addition of such points

CONCLUSION

Cape Verdeans are in a very interesting position today because of the 500th anniversary of Columbus' voyage to America. This situation will create a whole new industry in America that is completely untapped—that is, the development of Cape Verdean history and culture, which must be explained throughout America so that all Americans will be aware of Cape Verdeans.

It is incredible that everybody in America has heard of the Vietnamese and Cambodians, who have been here for less than two decades, but very few are aware of the Cape Verdeans, who have been here for centuries. Now we have a golden opportunity to tell the world who we are.

In some states, such as Texas, the Governor has already appointed a Director to head up the "Discovery of the New World" project to celebrate the 500th anniversary of Columbus. Anyone who is interested in promoting Cape Verdean culture during this period should contact their gubernatorial offices to find out what is being done about the Cape Verdean heritage during this project. I have also heard that the National Endowment for the Humanities in Washington, D.C., has millions of dollars allocated to this project. So everyone should pursue this very important project to ensure that Cape Verdeans are included and recognized.

To help overcome these barriers, I am now prepared to work together with anyone who is interested in finding solutions to this incredible problem. For example, there is a real need to coordinate seminars and workshops around the country. If we work together this could be a very important career field for the participants, reminiscent of the Affirmative Action programs. So, I will make myself available for any such venture. If you have any questions or suggestions, please write to me at:

Marcel Gomes Balla
Box 156
E. Wareham, MA 02538

IMPORTANT ADDRESSES OF CAPE VERDEAN CONTACTS

Europe:

Cafe des Arts
18 Place Emile Vandervelde
1000 Brussels, Belgium
tel: 512-1443

S.V.K. Travel Agency
Nieuwe Binnenweg 195-3021 GB
Rotterdam, Holland
tel: 010-477-8662

U.S.A.:

Cape Verdean (newspaper)
355 Main St.
Plymouth, MA 02367
tel: 617-585-1860

CVTP
Cape Verdean Television Productions
Box 9157
Pawtucket, RI 02860
tel: 401-723-7038

Fundonzinho Lounge
570 Dudley St.
Roxbury
Boston, MA
tel: 617-427-5401

United Social Club
480 South Front St.
New Bedford, MA
tel: 508-997-8526

C.V. Progressive Club
329 Governor St.
East Providence, RI
tel: 401-434-9012

Access International
International Business Consultants
Kathleen Barros

3870 La Sierra Ave., Ste 335
Riverside, CA 92503
tel: 714-247-7331

New World Enterprises, Ltd.
Manuel Lopes, Jr
Potomac Promenade
9812 Falls Rd., Ste 114
Potomac, MD 20854
tel: 301-279-8984

Kramer Associates, Inc.
Fermino J. Spencer
(Educator,International Services Consultant)
Washington, D.C. 20037
tel: 202-296-0230
fax: 202-296-6275

GMB Associates
Real Estate Services
Given Manuel Britto
605 E. Manchester Blvd.
Inglewood, CA 90301
tel: 213-419-1030

B. J. Enterprises
Barbara Gomes-Beach
(Marketing/Business Consultant, Fund Raising Activities)
P.O. Box "L"
Boston, MA 02119-0007
tel: 617-427-1838

Cape Verdean News
P.O. Box H - 3063
New Bedford, MA 02741

Antonio G. Correia (Translations, Immigration)
660 Morton St.
Mattapan, MA 02126
tel: 617-436-6298

C.V.S.C.
P.O. Box 8178
Los Angeles, CA 90008

— O NAVIO "MATILDE" —

Do seu pedestal, de porte orgulhoso e soberbo, Brava revivia ostensivamente sua vitoria sobre a fome de quarenta e dois. Corria o mes de Agosto—do ano de 1943—e o ano inspirava confianca.

Nas caras, outrora de expressao horripilante cintilavam agora uns olhos liquidos e confiantes. Aquilo que o ceu tenazmente vinha recusando anos alternados, durante multiplas geracoes, ali estava, mesmo ao pe aproximando montes e vales de modo profundo e inconfundivel permitindo a visao extasiar-se na contemplacao duma panoramica impar que percorria, suave, num verde e uniforme manto ate se confundir la em baixo com o azul e branco dum mar que subia ... subia ... arrastando atras de si sonhos e destinos, alegrias e lutos.

Mar! ... Que som mais doce e reconfortante para um coracao escravo e atraicoado?

La estava o "MATILDE" veleiro negro e surrado subindo-descendo; subindo-descendo, para, de cada vez que descesse beijar as aguas amenas da Baia de Faja d'Agua que procuravam furtar-se a sucessivos contactos indo refugiar-se na imensidao do oceano e nas areias da praia. O mastro de vante, o unico que lhe restava de tantas investidas contra o mar, parecia deleitar-se num continuo aceno ao ritmo suave do movimento bombordo-estibordo.

No conves, figuras de homens gesticulando, encostados a borda assistiam ruidosamente a chegada do bote "Elisabeth" que, gentilmente cedido pelo seu proprietario Viriato de Nho Djom de Pomba, vinha da Furna com mantimentos para abastecer o navio. A um canto, na proa, entre mil pensamentos e o conforto dum charuto americano, Daniel de Nho Ramos assistia impassivel a operacao de descarga. Depois desviava pesarosamente os olhos para dete-los demoradamente na silhueta do navio que se espalhava aqui e acola numa danca disforme e cintilante.

O sol ja ia a pique quando abandonou o seu posto.

Da terra continuava chegando mais carga dos passageiros. O "Santo Antao" dava uma ajudinha ao "Elisabeth." De regresso este levou Daniel a terra visivelmente contrariado pela demora dos restantes passageiros. O sol ja estava mesmo em cima da cabeca do "padre."

Defronte da Alfandega um grupo razoavel de curiosos seguia minuciosamente os acontecimentos. A retaguarda, a uma certa distancia, um outro grupo parecia conspirar. (fazia parte do grupo Djany, Abel, Djedji, todos irmaos de Daniel e como ele, tambem socios na compra do barco e organizadores da viagem; Toy, Jose, Manel da familia Balla de Santa Barbara, igualment socios.)

Foi para este que Daniel se encaminhou. Disse qualquer coisa que ninguem entendeu e todos se puseram a andar. A meio caminho porem, cruzaram com Nho Henrique de Lola, capitao de longo curso, que por sinal os procurava. Trazia um papel branco na mao que abanava com gosto ao mesmo tempo que explicava fugazmente como conseguira "cravar" das autoridades portuarias a falsa autorizacao de saida que despachava o barco para Praia—a intencao era partir para America com barco despachado para Praia.

Todavia entre gargalhadas e leves batidas nas costas la conseguiram chegar ao "barzinho" da aldeis, onde reinava grande animacao. Todos os passageiros—cinquenta ao todo— estavam ali reunidos, cada um despedindo da terra-mae a sua moda; os noivos entre namoricos e lagrimas refrescavam promessas; os casados as mulheres presentes prometiam nao esquecer dos pedidos dos miudos e de las tambem e aqueles que nao tinham parentes nem derentes, arrumados a um canto reconchegavam o estomago, com sucessivos "djabis" entre amigos da aldeia.

O relogio marcava 18 e 30 e o sol ja se tinha recolhido atras da ponta do padre. Nho Henrique ordenou o embarque. Mandou Nho Cristiano e Pulam certificar se os botes estavam em ordem.

Uma partida custa muito! Via-se isto, nitidamente em todos os rostos daqueles que iam partir. Uma fila long movimentava-se pesadamente na direccao do local designado para o embarque. Parecia num enterro; ninguem falava.

Por fim um cavaquinho distante velo quebrar a monotonia do ambiente com a morna "Hora di bai." Todas as vozes se uniram numa sinfonia triste. Chegados ao verso "o alma bibo quem qui al lebabo" as vozes femininas foram as primeiras a abandonar a parada. Vozes dispersas ainda se estorcavam por chegar ao fim, para morrerem pouco depois.

E dificil descrever uma partida. E comovente. Eis tudo.

Pelas vinte e tres horas o capitao mandou subir a vela e entregou o leme ao Nho Cristiano.

Entre o silencio da noite e a confianca dos seus hospedes, "Matilde" iniciava mais uma odisseia com o rumo tracado...America!?

Nota:

Embora o tempo tenha confirmado o destino do "Matilde" nao e de espantar que ainda hoje alguns bravenses, principalmente familiares que partiram, acreditem estar vivos seus familiares, algures no mundo.

Como estava-se num periodo de guerra—2d Guerra Mundial—varias suposicoes surgiram, todas elas tentando precisar o destino do barco.

Uns achavam que tinha sido afundado por algum navio de guerra solitario no Atlantico. Outros, por algum ciclone, pois, no mesmo dia da partida tinha havido temporal na Brava. Outros ainda sustentavam ter o barco atingido determinado ponto das costas Americanas como Brasil, Bermudas, costa de California, etc.

Mas o que realmente convenceu o povo de que tinha havido um naufragio foi o facto duma senhora do Lem ter sonhado com o filho—um dos passageiros—que lhe dizia terem sido engolidos pelo mar tres dias depois da partida. Isto e valido para quem acredita em telepatias...mas...uma outra que ainda vive—mora em Nova Sintra—argumenta ter visto pessoalmente tinha ela 19 anos, uma carta destinada ao pai dentro duma garrafa, por intermedio dum capitao estrangeiro que vinha parar a Praia.

Na carta tinham dado a posicao do barco. Segundo os calculos este deveria estar proximo de Bermudas.

Talvez os calculos estivessem errados . . .

THE BOAT "MATILDE"

The sun was already just above the head of the "padre."

From her pedestal, in a proud and splendid demeanor, Brava proudly remembers her victory over the famine of 1942. It happened in August 1943—the year that inspired confidence.

On their faces, they once had a horrifying expression, now their eyes are settled and confident. It is here that providence came tenaciously to deny them year after year, for several generations, it was right there in front of you, approaching the mountains and valleys in a profound and unmistakable way allowing an ecstatic vision of a panoramic oddity that passed by softly in a green and uniform cloak until it met below with the blue and white of the rising sea—rising ... while pulling behind itself the dreams, destinies, happiness and struggles. The sea! ... What is sweeter and more reassuring for a slavish and betrayed heart?

There stood the "Matilde," a black sailboat bouncing up and down, up and down; each time it came down kissing the pleasant waters of Faja d'Agua which was trying to escape out into the refuge of the immense sea and away from the seashore. The forward mast, the only one left after so many encounters with the sea, seemed to enjoy the continuous call of the soft swaying movement from side to side.

On the deck men were gesturing as they leaned against the railing amidst the noise and waited for the arrival of the boat "Elizabeth" which was kindly loaned by its owner Viriato de Nho Djom de Pomba who came from Furna with provisions to supply the boat. In one corner of the ship near the bow, deep in thought and enjoying an American cigar, was Daniel de Nho Ramos, expressionless and watching the unloading operation. After sadly shifting his eyes and stopping for a long time at the silhouette of the boat which bounced around here and there in an ugly and scintillating dance. The sun had almost reached its highest point, when he left his place.

On shore, more passenger cargo was still arriving. The "Saint Anthony" gave a little bit of help to the "Elizabeth." On returning to shore, Daniel became visibly annoyed by the delay of the other passengers. The sun was already just above the head of the "padre." (The "padre" is a natural rock formation that resembles a priest who is looking over the edge of the sea. The rock formation juts out into the sea at the very end of the harbor, hence the name, "Ponte de Padre" is given to this spot).

In front of the customs office, there was a sizable group of curious people meticulously following the events. In the rear, in the distance, another group seemed to be conspiring. This part of the group consisted of Djany, Abel, Djedje, all brothers of Daniel and, like him, they were also shareholders in the purchase of the boat and organizers of the trip; Toy, Jose, and Mane from the Balla family of Santa Barbara, Brava and equal shareholders. It was for this that Daniel went to them.

He said something that no one understood and everyone just kept on walking. Halfway up the path, however, they met with Nho Henrique de Lola, the Captain with many years of experience, who signaled and looked at them. Carrying a white paper in his hand, which he was waving with joy at the same time that he was quickly explaining how he was able to get the port authorities to "fix" a false departure authorization that would dispatch the boat to Praia—the intention was to leave for America with the boat dispatched to Praia (the capitol city on the island of Sao Tiago).

Also amid bursts of laughter and backslapping, they were gathering at the village bar, where they were having a good time. All of the passengers—50 in all—were there together, each one saying good-bye to the motherland in their own way: fiances, between hugging and tears, renewing their promises; the husbands of the women present, promised not to forget the requests of the youngsters; those who did not have relatives gathered in a corner amongst village friends while filling their stomachs with "djabis" (a local drink).

The time was now 6:30 p.m. and the sun had already disappeared behind the "Ponta do Padre." Nho Henrique gave the order to embark. He sent Nho Christiano and Pulam to certify that the boats were in order. The departure was very painful. It showed clearly in the faces of those who were leaving. A long procession moved sadly toward the departure point. It was like a funeral, nobody was talking.

Finally, a ukelele in the distance began to break up the monotonous atmosphere with the morna "Hora de bai" (a morna is a song in Crioulo and usually very sad). All of the voices were united in a sad symphony. When they reached the verse "O almo bibo quem qui al lebabo" (O living soul, who dares to take you away?), the female voices were the first to stop singing. The dispersing voices were still trying to reach the end, as they faded away shortly thereafter.

It is difficult to describe the departure as it was very touching. Everything was there.

By eleven o'clock in the evening, the Captain ordered the sails be raised and delivered the helm to Nho Cristiano. Amid the silence of the night and the confidence of the guests, the "Matilde" was initiating one more adventure with her course charted for America!

Note:

Even though time has confirmed the fate of the "Matilde," it is not surprising that still today, some Bravans, namely family members who were left behind, might still believe that their family members are still alive somewhere in the world.

Since it was during a time of war—World War II—various suspicions have been suggested, all of them to determine the boat's fate. Some believe that it had been sunk by a solitary warship in the Atlantic. Others, by a cyclone, since, on the day of departure, there had been a storm in Brava. Others still maintain that the boat reached a specific landfall on one of the American coasts, such as Brazil, Bermuda, the California coast, etc. ...

But what really convinced the people that the ship had been wrecked was based on a woman from Lem, who had a dream about her son, who was one of the passengers—he told her that they were swallowed up by the sea three days after they departed.[1] This is valid for those who believe in telepathy—but—another woman, who is still living and residing in Nova Sintra, states that when she was 19 years old she had personally seen a letter that was inside a bottle and addressed to her father that was sent by a foreign Captain's representative who came and stopped in Praia. In the letter, they had given the boat's location. According to these calculations it would have been in the vicinity of Bermuda.[2] Perhaps these calculations were in error ...

---

[1] In speaking with my friend Olavo, he explained to me this story about the woman who had a vision. According to this version of the story, the woman was still alive in 1986 and still tells this story, but she is not considered to be a stable person and suffers from psychotic problems, so nobody pays too much attention to her. Nevertheless, since she had her vision only three days after the boat departed, her story is even more dramatic.

[2] I remember once many years ago that a friend of mine had told me of an unusual story that he said was reported in "Ebony," a black-oriented magazine. The story had claimed that there existed a strange settlement of dark-skinned people who settled in a community in the vicinity of Baltimore, Maryland. These people supposedly spoke and acted different than typical U.S. blacks, but they apparently had difficulty in explaining the background of their community. Although my memory is vague about this story, I do remember him saying something about them arriving off the eastern U.S. coast as the result of a shipwreck while sailing to America. It seemed as though he may have met some of these people and they were supposedly Cape Verdeans. At the time I had heard this story, I had not known the details of the "Matilde," so I didn't pay too much attention to it. Unfortunately, my

friend has since died, so it would be very difficult to follow up on such a story.

I did, however, mention this story to my aunt, but she was convinced that the "Matilde" ended in disaster, because her brothers would certainly have contacted her or her mother if they had survived or any other survivors would have contacted someone in Cabo Verde.

[3] I remember also that Olavo had mentioned to me that one young boy had jumped off the boat and swum back to shore. He thought it was my cousin, but he wasn't sure, so I forgot about it. I learned later that my cousin, Humberto Balla, who was a son of Belmiro Balla, was 12 years old at the time and that he became frightened on the boat as it was sailing away, so he jumped off and swam back to Faja d'Agua. He apparently became frightened when he saw the boat was leaking. Once he returned to shore, after a half hour swim, he sat and cried while watching the boat disappear out of sight. I mentioned this to a cousin who lives in Massachusetts and he said that Humberto Balla is his nephew and lives in Praia, Sao Tiago. Today he should be almost 60 years old.

Unfortunately, I did not get to talk to him personally when I was in Praia, but I found the story later in the book *Cape Verdeans in America—Our Story*.

The author of this story is unknown, but I was given a copy of it while in Brava. The translation is my own, with some help from a cousin.

There are other stories that are told about the boats and their crews during the days of the "Brava Packet Trade." These stories will attest to the courage and heroism of the Cape Verdeans as they bought and sailed their own boats, while risking their lives in their struggle against the sea, to reach the shores of America, while never forgetting the loved ones they left behind. Many such stories are described in *Cape Verdeans in America—Our Story*, published in 1978 by TCHUBA and the American Committee for Cape Verde, Inc., 14 Beacon St., Boston, MA 02108. They also offer a Teacher's Guide, for use with their book, upon request.

MATILDE

1 — Partem os filhos da Brava
Dignos irmaos de os de outrora
Causa que entao os levara
E a mesma que os leva agora
E nada evita a partida
De quem quer vencer na vida

Velas ao vento
Navio ao largo
Que triste amargo
No lento

2 — Partem p'ra longe
Partem chorando
Partem com fe
Ai ate quando

Velas a vento
Navio ao largo
Que triste amargo
No lento

3 — Choram saudades da terra
Que os seus amores encerra
Maes, esposas, bens, amadas
Nao choreis vossos amores
Nao de mais nem as lufadas
Nem das ondas ferozes
Que tem mais forca vontade
Que a alma da tempestade
O Ceu ao lado todo incorberto
E esta por certo na gloria

Partem p'ra longe
Partem chorando
Partem saudosos
Saudades deixando

Velas ao vento
Navio ao largo
Que triste amargo
No lento
E assim vao sulcando o mar
Pensando sempre em voltar

Silvestre Faria

131

Do not cry for your loved ones anymore, Neither are the gusts of winds, nor the ferocious waves.

MATILDE

1 — The sons of Brava are leaving
The dignified brothers
Of those from long ago
For the cause that they had then
Is the same that takes them today
And nothing eludes the departure
Of those who desire to succeed in life.

Sails into the wind
The ship is sailing away
How sadly prepared
Slowly she goes.

2 — They are going far away
Departing with tears
Leaving with faith
Alas! Until whenever.

Sails into the wind
The ship is sailing away
How sadly prepared
Slowly she goes.

3 — Grieving for the homeland
Which holds their loved ones.
Mothers, wives and loved ones,
Don't cry for your loved ones anymore.
Neither are the gusts of winds
Nor the ferocious waves
That have a more powerful will
Than the soul of the storm.
In heaven at the side of the
Almighty.
And there, for certain,
They are in splendor.

They are going far away,
They are leaving and grieving,
They are leaving and yearning,
Leaving with nostalgia for the Motherland.

Sails into the wind,
The ship is sailing away,
How sadly prepared,
Slowly she goes;
And as soon as they cross the sea,
They think always of returning.

133

HORA DE BAI

Hora de bai,
Hora de dor,
Ja'n q're
Pa el ca manche
De cada bez
Que 'n ta lembra,
Ma'n q're
Fica 'n morre

Hora de bai,
Hora de dor
Amor,
Dixa 'n tchora
Corpo catibo,
Ba bo que e escrabo
O alma bibo,
Quem que al lebabo?

Se bem e doce,
Bai e magoado;
Mas, se ca bado,
Ca ta birado
Se no morre
Na despedida,
Nhor Des na volta
Ta dano bida.

Dixam tchora
Destino de home:
Es dor
Que ca tem nome:

Dor de cretcheu,
Dor de sodade
De alguem
Que'n q're, que q'rem ...

Dixam tchora
Destino de home,
Oh Dor
Que ca tem nome
Sofri na vista
Se tem certeza,
Morre na ausencia,
Na bo tristeza.

—Eugenio Tavares

HORA DI BAI

Hour of departure,
Hour of grief.
Would that it
Might never dawn!
Every time I remember it,
I want to
Lie down and die!

Hour of departure,
Hour of grief!
My love,
Let me weep!
Captive body,
Go thou, slave!
O living soul,
Who dares to take you away?

If coming home is sweet
Departing is bitter.
Yet, if one doesn't leave
One can never return.
If we die
Saying a farewell
God, on our return
Will give us our life.

Leave me to mourn
The destiny of man'
This grief
Which has no name!

Lover's despair
This painful longing
For someone
Whom I love and who loves me.

Leave me to mourn
The destiny of man
O Grief
Which has no name!
I would rather suffer
Being close to you
Than die far away alone and
Engulfed in sorrow.

CAPE VERDEAN FACTS

**Uninhabited volcanic islands discovered circa 1456 by Portugal—16° N, 24° W.

**First settlement circa 1462.

**Along with the Azoreans and Madeirans, Cape Verdeans became the first settlers in a New World in the 15th century.

**First foothold of Christianity beyond the "Old World" of Europe and the Middle East.

**First international trade agreement authorized by Portugal in 1466 for the trading of merchandise and slaves in Guinea, Gambia and "Cap de Mont" (now Liberia).

**1495—becomes a part of Portugal.

**June 27, 1498—Columbus calls at Cape Verde for logistical support during voyage to America and is given instructions for finding South America by Cape Verdeans.

**1500—Pedro Alvarez Cabral goes to Cabo Verde to make plans to "officially" discover Brazil.

**1580-1640—Cabo Verde became part of the Spanish Kingdom under King Phillip II of Spain.

**Cape Verdean slave traders were called *lancados*.

**During the late 15th century and early 16th century Cabo Verde was generally regarded as the most important calling port for all the great navigators such as Diaz, Vasco da Gama, Magellan, Columbus and Cabral. Logistical support was provided by Cape Verdeans, which enabled these navigators to discover the Americas and a new sea route to India and around the world.

**Many seamen from the Old World and slaves from Africa settled the islands to form a new race of people known as mestizos or Crioulos and now Cape Verdeans. These people became the glue that held the Portuguese Empire together.

**Many of the inhabitants eventually settled in Europe, America, Brazil and Africa because of frequent droughts and famine on the islands.

**July 5, 1975—Cape Verde becomes independent from Portugal.

**After being ruled by a one-party system since independence, a multi-party system and free elections have been authorized for 1990.

**The total world population of Cape Verdeans is less than 1 million with the majority (375,000) in Cabo Verde and about 350,000 in the U.S.A. and 70,000 in Portugal. There are also large settlements in Luxembourg and Holland and scattered settlements in Belgium, France, Italy, Spain and Brazil as well as in Africa and Asia.

**Cape Verdeans are an international people united by a common homeland and culture based on language, cuisine, music and suffering.

**Cape Verdeans are very sensitive towards the racial classification systems that exist in America and South Africa. This is not a Cape Verdean problem, but rather an American or South African problem.

**Cape Verdeans were the primary ethnic group that developed the Ocean Spray Cranberry industry in Onset, Massachusetts. It is very unlikely that the Ocean Spray Company could have been successful without Cape Verdeans because of the Cape Verdean work ethic and dedication.

**The capital of Cabo Verde is Praia (population: 58,000—1989 est.) on the island of Sao Tiago. There are 10 major islands.

**The official language is Portuguese. Many Cape Verdeans also speak Crioulo, a mixture of Portuguese and African dialects.

**Antonio Cardozo (1904-84) a Cape Verdean and prominent Boston attorney, was the very first student to enroll at the Fletcher School of International Law and Diplomacy in 1933 at Tufts University, Boston, MA. He was also the first Fletcher graduate to receive the Distinguished Service Award from the Alumni Council.

CAPE VERDEAN
ACHIEVEMENTS OF
HISTORICAL SIGNIFICANCE

1. Cape Verdeans, along with the Madeirans and Azoreans were the first Christian settlers in a new world, which became the basis for the discovery of America.

2. Cotton was produced and cultivated by African slaves in Cabo Verde (Fogo) years before Columbus discovered America. Cape Verdean technology in the cotton industry was later copied and introduced to America, which culminated in the "Civil War" that changed the course of Amerian history.

3. Cape Verdeans were directly involved in the opening of a "sea route" to India in 1497.

4. Cape Verdeans provided important assistance and advice to Columbus.

5. Cape Verdeans were direct participants in the Discovery of Brazil in 1500.

6. Cape Verdeans provided direct support and assistance in the final phase of Magellan's voyage around the world which proved that the world was round.

7. Cape Verdeans supplied the first Brazilian settlements in the 16th century with horses, cows, sheep, goats and oxen.

8. African yams, rice shoots and sugar cane were transferred from the "Old World" via Cabo Verde to Brazil.

9. Once a certain amount of vital food bearing plants and animals had been transferred to Brazil by Cape Verdeans, the diffusion became self-perpetuating.

10. Brazilian manioc plants and corn were introduced into Africa via Cabo Verde.

11. Brazilian social customs were imitated from Cabo Verde and Sao Tome.

12. In the 17th century, Cabo Verde governed an area along the African coast which extended from the south of Morocco down to Sierra Leone.

13. In the 17th century, Cape Verdeans also supplied horses to the English possessions of the West Indies.

DECLARATION OF CAPE VERDEAN UNITY & RIGHTS

We, the Cape Verdean people of America and the world, declare to all nations:

Article I
That we are members of the human race.

Article II
That no nation has the right to classify us by the tone of our skin.

Article III
That we are also Americans, with equal rights.

Article IV
That we must now tell America and the world that we are a unique, united and proud people.

Article V
That we do not rely on documents bestowed on us by others as proof of our rights and freedoms; which are our birthrights inherited from a Supreme Authority and thus cannot be denied us by any man or nation.

Article VI
That the time has come for Cape Verdeans to unite and educate others as to the role we played in the history of the world and become duly recognized.

Article VII
That no man is free, lest he takes control of himself and masters his own destiny and so it should be with the Cape Verdeans of the world, that lest we take control of our own destiny, we can never be free.

NATIONAL ANTHEM OF CABO VERDE

This is Our Beloved Country
Sun, Sweat, Green Sea
Centuries of pain and hope
This is the land of our ancestors!
Fruit of our hands
The flower of our blood
This our beloved Country!

Long live our beloved country
Fly in the sky the flag of our
  struggle
Against the foreign yoke!

We shall build in our immortal
  homeland
Peace and progress.

Branches of the same trunk
Eyes to the same light
This is the strength of our
  union
Sing the sea and the land
The Dawn and the Sun
That our struggle has borne
  fruit.

Esta E A Nossa Patria Amada
Sol, Suor e o Verde Mar
Seculos de dor e esperanca
Esta e a terra dos nossos avos!
Fruto das nossas maos
Da flor do nosso sangue
Esta e a nossa patria amada!

Viva a patria gloriosa
Floriu nos ceus a bandeira
  da luta
Cor-Avante contra o jugo
  estrangeiro!
Bis-Nos vamos constuir na patria
  imorta
A paz e o progresso.

Ramos do mesmo tronco
Olhos na mesma luz
Esta e a forca da nossa
  uniao
Cantem o mare'e a terra
A madrugada e o Sol
Que a nossa luta fecundou.

REFERENCES

Admiral of the Ocean Sea, by Samuel Eliot Morison, 1942.

The Story of the Americas, by Leland Dewitt Baldwin, 1943.

They Came Before Columbus, by Ivan Van Sertim, 1976.

Spain in America, by Charles Gibson, 1966.

The European Discoveries of America, by Samuel Eliot Morison, 1972.

The Shaping of America, Vol. 1 Atlantic America 1492-1800, by D. W. Meinig, 1986.

Harvard Encyclopedia of American Ethnic Groups, Harvard University Press, 1980.

Historia de Portugal, A. H. de Oliveira Marques, 1972

The Portuguese Pioneers, by Edgar Prestage, 1933.

The Cape Verde Islands, by Richard Lebban and Marilyn Halter, 1987.

The Atlantic Islands, by T. Bentley Duncan, 1973.

Le Moulin est Le Pilon, by Nelson Eurico Cabral, 1980.

EPILOGUE

Unknown to most Americans is the fact that Cape Verdeans represented the historical focal point for transferring "Old World" values and culture to the "New World". Numerous animals and plants were introduced to the New World by Cape Verdeans many years before the English arrived on American shores. Perhaps America will now realize that in order to better understand American history, Americans will need to learn something about Cape Verdean history and finally to recognize the Cape Verdean people as being a distinct and unique people with a proud heritage.